What to Expect When You're No

A No Nonsense Discussion About Infertility.

Hollie Page.

This book is dedicated to every couple dealing with infertility. You are all my heroes.

Hx

Introduction

Raise your hand if like me you've been asked THAT QUESTION:

"When are you going to have children?"

Now, this question may seem completely innocent to some, and to most people, it is harmless. But to others, like me, it is quite possibly the one question we loathe being asked (more so than "whose turn is it to do the dishes?"). Why? Because for some of us, it's not an easy one to answer. Hopefully, this book will help you to understand why, and to those who still don't know quite how to answer it, hopefully it will help you too.

First and foremost, I don't want this to sound like I'm whining, or whinging, or claiming life's not fair.

This is an account, first hand and with the help of some lovely women and men I have had the great fortune of getting to know. They are going to help explain what it is like being a 30 something year old who hasn't got children, in a time in our lives where it seems it is customary to ask any 30 something woman in a stable relationship the question some of us dread:

"When are you going to have kids?"

It seems to me wherever I look these days someone I know is either pregnant or has just had a baby. I've just sat and watched a programme on TV where a woman gave birth to twins while the father of her children's ex-partner (who, by the way, also carried one of his children – I can't keep up with American rom coms) is there with her. I'm also currently checking my phone every 6 minutes waiting for the news that my best friend has had her first baby (FYI, baby girl, 6lbs, gorgeous). I'm also an auntie to five gorgeous little humans, courtesy of my sister. They're the best. Fact. I'm not a baby hater.

This last year alone, I've seen 8 "we're having a baby!" posts, and to date, 9 of my friends have had children in that time. (I suspect this is something to do with the summer of sports we had in 2016, with the Euros and the Olympics in Rio, as well as the usual cricket, tennis etc. well timed, gents.) Three people at my work are currently pregnant (well, 2, one of them is a 22-year-old boy who "accidentally" got his girlfriend pregnant. Because that's a thing too now). When I scroll through my social media, if it's not a baby bump swelling underneath a beautiful summer shirt, new-born photos, or pictures of adorable little humans pushing raspberries into their gorgeous chubby little cheeks, it's a pee on a stick photo, a well-crafted celebrity selfie announcement, or some other elaborate and adorable announcement. Why does this bother you so much! I hear you cry! Well, that's because for some of us, it's not as easy to fall pregnant as others.

I won't give you the backstory of events that lead to this outcome, you'll hear about that in the chapters to come, but let's just say I'm what the doctor's class as "fertility challenged". I have what is classed as a broken reproductive system, and only have one ovary, which automatically gives me 50% less chance of getting pregnant.

Add to that the Fallopian tube scarring and the scar tissue from a laceration in my womb and that percentage drops even further. It doesn't mean I can't have kids, which is great, it does mean that my partner and I will have to do a lot of planning, undergo a lot of testing, and be referred to a medical professional to help us have babies. You know when you hear people say their kids were a surprise, and they just popped up out of nowhere? Yeah, that won't be us. Our kids will be meticulously planned for around 2 years (one of those years is what they class as the trying to conceive period), so there will be no surprises there.

But is that a good thing? Do we talk about it enough? Isn't it straight forward? Does it work every time? I don't think so. The reason I am writing this, is because as I've grown up, I always knew that one day I would want to have a family. But no one has ever told me just how hard it is. To go through your 20's and arrive on the metaphorical eve of what some people call your defining decade, and still not know very much more about the processes of assisted fertility treatments, how much of a ball ache it is, and the heartache that comes along with it. So along with my own personal experiences this project/book/ whatever it turns out to be, will include some stories from some very lovely ladies and gents. They are awesome because they have opened up about what they are going through or have gone through in the quest for what most see as being the most natural thing in the world. There will be laughs, there will be tears, but hopefully you will find this helpful. And I'll try to keep it as light-hearted as I can.

Act One - No, we are not having a baby.

So, let me formally introduce myself to you, my dear reader. I'm 30 years old, I have good job, a nice house, a cat, a dog, and a boyfriend – how school playground does that sound? Can I call him my man friend? No? OK. We have been together for just over 2 years, and on our first date, I drunkenly blurted out to him that I might not be able to have children without the aid of a test tube. I know, I know, who does that? (me, apparently).

Luckily, he did not run off and leave me sitting there, staring into the bottom of my empty wine glass, and is hugely supportive and understanding about the whole thing. Previously my relationships have been defined by this one characteristic. Ridiculous, right? They varied in different reasons why but had the same theme. Because my reproductive system is flawed, they no longer saw me as a lifelong companion. One relationship lasted three years until this was a problem, others, a couple of weeks, but regardless it was horrible to be told that because it might be difficult, they would decide you weren't worth it. I don't think there is much else that could be as hurtful.

Obviously, it was for the best as my man is incredible. He doesn't (seem to) mind that much that our family will require some forward planning, and this year we intend to "start trying but not be trying" as some people put it. Should nothing happen after about a year, we then get to go through the laborious task of fertility treatment. Neither of us knows what this will involve, as until we go for those tests, we don't really know what the root of the problem is. Until then, whenever someone asks, "are you two planning on starting a family soon?" we must come up with some sort of explanation. Here lies my first biggest bug bear of being almost 30 and not having kids. The constant questioning, and basically being nosey when it comes to people's personal business.

Where a lot of people share their pregnancy announcement stories on social media, I share photos of my cat and dog. When people ask me "so, are you and the man going to get married and have kids?" I tactfully change the subject away from us and onto something else. When my colleagues complain about how annoying their kids are, I smile and go back to my work. When my best friend announced that she and her husband were expecting their first baby, I got a pang of jealously, followed swiftly by guilt. And then I felt so happy for them I thought I was going to burst.

For me, and many others, all of the above can literally make your blood boil, your palms sweat, and make you feel so many emotions at once it makes you wonder how you manage to keep them all contained.

I've been in a room of people I've barely met and been met with the statement, "Still no kids? That's quite unusual for someone your age - you best get a move on!". My response varies depending on the person, and the situation, but it usually includes forced smiles and restraint, no matter how much I want to tell them to piss off with their opinion. I can't blame them, but it still hurts. Mainly because they don't know that I've already had 2 "chemical pregnancies". That's when you have a miscarriage in the very early stages, around 4-6 weeks.
Some women don't even realize they have been pregnant. It's like the worst period you can ever imagine, plus utter heartbreak over someone you didn't even know you could love. Almost like an elephant is doing a dance on your uterus while someone sets off a corkscrew in your cervix. And at the same time, a teaspoon can make you cry. The first time I cried silently for days. I didn't want to cry in front of Tim, because I didn't want him to see how upset I was. It was the most horrific experience I have ever been through. On the surface, I was just Hollie, going on as normal I tried to push it to the back of my mind and throw myself into work. Because the other option was grieving, which made me feel like a failure, and trust me, I already feel like that most of the time. On the inside my world was crumbling.

The day I got a faint line on a stick, I was terrified, nervous, excited, and for a week I fell in love with the human that could have grown inside me. I found myself daydreaming about the perfect little family we would have, and it made me so happy, even if I was shitting myself at the thought. We had only been together for 10 months when this happened. We had even discussed about when we would tell our parents, and how we would tell our friends. Then on the Friday evening, exactly 8 days after my period was due, I have the most sickening cramps, I felt lightheaded and nauseous, and once I saw the bright red blood, as dramatic as it sounds, I felt empty. The weekend came and went with a blur, and I tried my hardest to cover up the feelings of loss and the pain. I tried to put on a brave face, whatever that is, to mask my disappointment from my partner - I felt like I was such a let-down. Why would anyone want to plan a future with someone like me if I can't even reproduce? I just wanted this feeling of loss to be over.

On the Monday lunchtime, I went to the doctors, and they confirmed to me that I was no longer pregnant and had indeed had an early miscarriage. But that I should be happy because this means I CAN get pregnant. Oh yay, tell me that now why don't you. Never mind that my hormones have been fired into a blender that is my nervous system. I'm in agony, and you can clearly see in my medical notes that I have had depression and suffer with anxiety. Very tactful. (In writing this book, I took some comfort in the knowledge that I am not the only one who feels the NHS could do with being a bit more sympathetic and sensitive towards women in our position).

But anyway, you just have to move on, otherwise the feelings of loss and sadness can completely consume you. The second time it happened a couple of months later, I knew the signs, so I didn't feel the need to go to the doctors, so I didn't. I stayed home and hugged a hot water bottle and waited for it to pass, because that's all I could do. It didn't make it any less difficult or emotional or made me feel any less useless, but at that moment crying over it doesn't really seem like an option. I had to keep telling myself "It was hardly even a ball of cells. It wasn't anything".

I've cried a lot about not being able to have kids you see, for a lot of reasons. These include:

- *Because my sister has five children and they are the most amazing humans I have ever met. They make my heart want to explode because they are so adorable. If you met them you would understand.*

- *Because my mum and sister get on at me for not having any kids. Apparently, my nieces and nephews, despite there being five of them, they need cousins. No idea why, to form a football team maybe?*

- *Because my partner would be an amazing dad, and I worry constantly that he will go back on what he said on our first date and want kids with someone with a fully functioning womb. He hasn't, and I love him unconditionally because of it. Amongst many other things (he's also an amazing cook, he's funny, he's sweet, he's creative and clever, you get the picture).*

- *Because previous boyfriends have done that exact thing. Apparently, it is a higher priority for men that we are led to believe. Shock horror ladies - men do want to settle down and have kids, despite what the internet tells you. I mean, unless they were using this as an excuse? In which case to all my ex's and to the guys I dated that dealt the biggest blow to my self-esteem by telling me that "it's not me, it's you" based on the absence of my ovary - thanks guys, it's all worked out fine for me.*

- *Because my friend got pregnant, she didn't invite me to her baby shower because she thought it would upset me. (She felt the need to message me and tell me this. Not even face to face. Needless to say, we are not really friends anymore). What upset me is that she thought me being in the presence of her bump meant I would have a breakdown. I don't cry over baby bumps - I cry because there's no Nutella left in the jar three days before Aunt Flo comes around to town.*

- *Because when I was out for lunch one day, someone I used to work with patted my stomach and asked how I was feeling, and assumed I was pregnant. Um, no, I'm not pregnant, I'm just bloated. Thanks for pointing that out to me though…. why do people think it's OK to assume? (Probably didn't help that I had two packets of Jaffa cakes in one hand and a cheese twist from M&S in the other.) I cried because I was humiliated, and I cried because I wanted to be able to say that I was having a baby, and I couldn't. And that sucks.*

- *Because one Sunday afternoon my next-door neighbour came to my door with a big handful of runner beans from her allotment for us, which was very sweet of her. We were chatting on the doorstep, and she then put both hands on my stomach and asked me if I was expecting. I told her no, and she replied with "oh, it's just you look noticeably different." The shock really threw me. As I smiled and said goodbye, I just started crying my eyes out. I then tried to hide this feeling from Tim, and went out on a 6-mile run because I felt fat and gross and hated myself because I wasn't pregnant. I pushed him away, and felt horrible about it - but in my head, who wants to "cuddle" with someone who looks pregnant but isn't and might not be able to? It's a real head fuck. I told him what happened and felt a little better, but moments like that can really fuck a person's head up. Please don't go around touching people's tummies - they might just have a pizza bloat, and it can be really fucking hurtful.*

- *Because every time I hear of one of my friends getting pregnant I feel jealous before I feel happy for them, and then I feel guilty. It's an emotional fucking roller coaster. The jealously and the guilt go away very quickly I might add, but the happiness I feel for them is unconditional. I think sometimes those who know our infertility struggles try and not tell us about these kinds of things. I just want to put it out there – unless we explicitly tell you we are hurt and upset that you are pregnant and don't want anything to do with you, don't shut us out. If you are a friend, trust me, we are so happy for you we could burst.*

I have often felt guilty for feeling like this, and then I get angry at myself and my body. Especially when my partner talks about how much he wants to start a family. It makes me feel like I'm a failure, like I can't give him the one thing he wants. I've said it before and I've said it again, he is incredibly supportive. Yet I still get this knot of anxiety in my stomach when I think about just how long it's going to take us, and even then, what if it doesn't work? These thoughts cripple you.

One piece of advice I can offer is to ensure that if you are feeling like this, you have to talk to those around you. Keeping everything bottled up will consume you, and it is not healthy to hold on to these negative feelings. I am speaking as someone who has suffered with the blackest, darkest days of depression, anxiety, suicidal thoughts and utter hatred for myself for many years.

There are loads of other times I felt emotional, guilty, and just a shit person because of my hostile reproductive system, and looking back, when I was 18 years old I wish I had taken the counselling I was offered to come to terms with "my condition". But back then I just wanted to forget about it. Who wants to think about that sort of thing at 18, when your whole life is ahead of you? I am incredibly lucky that I have some incredible friends who have been so supportive, who have listened to me whinge and cry and moan and whine and have basically been my therapists while I came to terms with everything, and still do to this day. (If you're reading this, I love you gals. You're the best.)

So back to those questions. In my wise older (30 years on this planet, I'm wise) years, I've adopted a slightly different approach. Based on my own experiences, I've basically becoming thicker skinned to these extremely personal and quite frankly inappropriate questions. To all those people who think it's perfectly fine to be so intrusive, I say this– are you really prepared for the answer to your question? But really, the next time you feel like being that nosey, what will you say to the woman who admits, "I can't have children? We've been trying for years." Queue awkward silences and muttered apologies. What about the woman who replies, "I've never wanted kids. Why are you asking me such a personal question?" It's simply not okay to bury your head in the sand and pretend like this is a benign question. It's not. It's really fucking personal and insensitive. So please, stop assuming that:

 A) all people want children
 B) all people want to give you a detailed rundown of their family planning and fertility struggles.

Anytime somebody asks me if I'm going to have kids, I'm tell them, 'One day, you're going to ask that to the wrong person. They might be really struggling, and it's going to be really hurtful to them." I hate that people think they have a right to know. It's not really anyone's business unless you let it be, and take it from me, if someone confides in you over something so personal; you must be a top human to them.

The top comment a lot of women like me get when we are asked by our friends and family, is "When are you going to start having children?" I'm not sure about you, but I don't think there is ever a right or wrong time to have kids. It can be extremely hurtful for someone to ask you this question, and it can be quite a difficult one to answer. Most of the time we just don't know if or when it will happen. If you've already been told that it's going to be even more difficult, it just feels like it's an uphill struggle. And then, should you decide to tell people ", we've been trying, and we might not be able to have kids", people go one of three ways: They ask you if you're going to adopt. Or ask if you are you going to have IVF? Or they change the subject. In this first chapter, I'd like to share with you some of the nitty gritty facts about infertility, pregnancy, and all the bells and whistles that go along with it. If you are in the same boat as me, hopefully this will help you to see you aren't the only one.

Fun Facts About Fertility (Or the Lack of)

Around 1 in 6 couples in the UK today have difficulty conceiving, and it is estimated to affect over 3.5 million people. THREE POINT FIVE MILLION. See - I told you you weren't alone. There's a few of us.

About 84% of couples will conceive naturally within one year if they have regular unprotected sex.

(Of all the sites I've looked at, no one seems to be able to tell me what "regular" means. 3 times a week? 5 times a week? Missionary? Who knows. I'd take a stab and say three times a week. Roughly.).

For every 100 couples trying to conceive the "normal" way:
- 84 will conceive within one year
- 92 will conceive within two years
- 93 will conceive within three years

For couples who have been trying for more than three years without success, the likelihood of pregnancy in the next year is 25% or less.

Primary infertility refers to couples who have not become pregnant after at least 1 year without using birth control methods.

Secondary infertility is defined as the inability to become pregnant, or to carry a pregnancy to term after the birth of one or more children. The birth of the first child won't have involved any assisted reproductive technologies or fertility medications.

Unexplained infertility is infertility that is idiopathic in the sense that its cause remains unknown. Even after an infertility assessment, usually including semen analysis in the man and assessment of ovulation and fallopian tubes in the woman,

What causes infertility?
There are many, many different potential causes of infertility, and fertility problems can affect both parties. However, it is not always possible to identify the cause, even after all the testing, they can come back to be completely inconclusive. Aka, unexplained infertility, which occurs in around 25% of couples.

The most common causes of infertility in women include irregular ovulation, a blockage of the fallopian tubes, PCOS and endometriosis. For the gents, poor quality of semen (or swimmers as I prefer to call them), blockages in tubes, and a low sperm count are the usual suspects.

Treatments can be as simple as medication in the form of injections or a daily tablet to stimulate egg production, such as clomid to artificial insemination or IUI (long needle, sperm put into the cervix) to full on IVF (In really simple terms eggs come out, sperm comes out, mix in a petri dish, put back into woman's womb). For men, as the problem lies in the process of either making or moving the sperm, the treatments that are available include clearing any plumbing blockages, hormonal treatments to ensure the right levels of testosterone are being produced to ensure it is healthy, and of course, Artificial insemination and IVF. I'll go into more detail about what these entail later.

Pregnancy and infertility: The facts and the Myths

Keeping your little swimmers cool helps maintain their health.
So long tight underwear. If you are trying to get pregnant, it's best to make sure your man is keeping his assets one or two degrees cooler than the rest of a man's body, so avoid tight underwear or clothes. Because we needed another reason to get rid of men's skinny jeans.

Isn't infertility a woman's problem only?
Heck no! This is a huge misconception. Both women and men can have problems that cause infertility. To give you the numbers, about one-third of infertility cases are caused by women's problems. Another one third of fertility problems are due to the man. The other cases are caused by a mixture of male and female problems or by unknown problems.

Obesity can affect ovulation.
More than 25 percent of women don't know that weight gain can have an impact on their ability to conceive. Excess weight may be associated with other health issues, such as thyroid problems and diabetes. These can affect your fertility. If you are having abnormal or irregular periods (like cycles that last more than 35 days), you may not be ovulating every month, making you less likely to become pregnant

The good news: If you are overweight, losing five to 10 percent of your body weight can improve your chances of conception. If you haven't conceived after 12 months of trying, make an appointment to see your GP.

It's harder to become pregnant as you get older.
One-fifth of women don't realize that aging affects their odds of becoming pregnant.
At 30-years-old, you have a 20 percent chance of becoming pregnant each cycle, and the likelihood shrinks to 5 percent per cycle by the time you're 40. There's also a greater risk of miscarriage and birth defects as you age. If you're over age 35, see your doctor if you're not pregnant after six months of trying.

Your sense of smell skyrockets when you're ovulating.
I am not kidding, you read that right. If you've been smelling funny things all day, it could mean it's prime baby-making time. So instead of complaining about his overwhelming BO after he hits the gym, maybe take it as a cue to, ahem, "cuddle" After a shower.

You only have a 15-percent chance of conceiving each month.
When you've been TTC (that's Trying to Conceive) for a while, it's hard not to notice all the pregnant women who seem to be popping up with their bumps everywhere. But the fact is, couples in their thirties having unprotected sex only have a 15-percent chance of conceiving each month. It usually takes about eight months until you get a Big Fat Positive. (One study also claimed that most couples have sex about 104 times before seeing a positive pee stick.) So, keep the facts in mind before you get discouraged.

You're (even more) sexy when you're ovulating.
When British researchers asked a group of men to look through photos of 48 women and choose who they thought were the most beautiful, the results overwhelmingly showed men were more drawn to ovulating women. Most notably on their radar? The fuller lips, dilated pupils and softer skin tone of the women who were ovulating. Thank you, mother nature.

Myths Unravelled

Myth: Having sex every day will increase our chances of conceiving
Couples trying to get pregnant are encouraged to have intercourse regularly to increase their chances of conception, that's a no brainer. But doing the horizontal shuffle every day is likely to leave you exhausted, particularly as it takes many couples 6-12 months to conceive. Have a day off every now and again.

Myth: You can't get pregnant when you are on your period

Wrong. While women cannot conceive during menstruation (the hormones resulting in menstruation are the opposite of those required for a pregnancy to occur), you can conceive from sex during menstruation. You may ovulate early and sperm can survive for up to 5 days after release.

Myth: You can only conceive from sex on the day that you ovulate

Not true. The human egg is ready for fertilization for around 24 hours after it is released from the ovaries. Given that sperm can survive for up to 5 days after intercourse and women may produce more than 1 egg in a 24-hour period, technically a woman can conceive from intercourse occurring from anything up to 5 days prior to or even up to 2 days after ovulation.

Myth: A normal menstrual cycle is 28 days

Wrong again, this is in fact a myth perpetuated by the contraceptive pill which makes your cycles regular and 28 days in length. In fact, menstrual cycles can vary from anything between 24-36 days, and not only vary between women but can vary considerably in any individual woman from month to month. Mine for example, can be anything from 26 days to 37 days, and it's fucking frustrating.

Myth: Lying down with legs raised after sex will increase chances of getting pregnant

While there is no scientific evidence to support this, some people claim it helps get the sperm going in the right direction. (But given they are given a pretty good run up, it's not completely necessary) It is totally harmless it has to be worth a shot, if you'll pardon the pun.

Myth: Eating oysters will boost fertility
There is an infinitesimal grain of truth in this one, because oysters are a rich source of zinc, low levels of which can be a factor in hampering fertility. But, you should really take stock of your diet and ensure that you are eating plenty of fruit and vegetables, wholegrain cereals, which are rich in antioxidants, include oily types of fish twice each week (e.g. salmon, herring, sardine, etc) to boost essential fatty acid and cut down on caffeine and alcohol both of which can hinder conception if taken in excess. Don't forget to keep active and if you are a smoker, quit. This goes for men too.

Myth: You can get everything you need from diet and don't need to take supplements
This is definitely not true. In fact, all women are advised to take a supplement containing 400mcg of folic acid daily while trying to conceive and for the first 3 months of pregnancy. Taking a folic acid supplement is important for neural tube development in the baby. Most of us don't manage to eat a perfect diet all the time, and even those of us who do eat well won't be getting the RDA of folic acid, so taking a supplement specifically tailored for conception or pregnancy can help to ensure that there are plenty of all the vitamins and minerals important for conception.

Are we leaving it too late?
According to research, women are leaving it later to start a family. The Office of National Statistics has reported that, since the 1980s, the rates for women giving birth at age 30 or over have gone up, while the rates for women giving birth aged under 30 have fallen. It's worth noting that fertility falls more sharply for women as they age than for men. Us ladies are at our most fertile between the ages of 20 and 24 years. As women grow older the likelihood of getting pregnant falls while the likelihood of infertility rises sharply. Men tend to remain fertile for much longer but male fertility still declines with age, although less dramatically.

Act Two - So you think it's easy? Think again!

So, you're doing everything right. You're taking supplements. You're exercising. You do yoga and try not to get stressed out, because for some reason everyone assumes that being relaxed means you get pregnant easier. It may surprise you, but stress has very little impact on your chances of getting pregnant. Unless you are experiencing high levels of stress every day. Normal day to day stresses such as running out of loo roll and being late for work don't really have an impact, so stop trying to be perfect and calm and serene - stress is good for you at times! Nothing is happening. So, you just go to the doctors, and get told that you need to be referred for testing. Simple, right?

Wrong.

Before you're even allowed to be considered for any sort of medical testing by your doctor, you will need to have been trying for at least a year (this is reduced if you have already been diagnosed with a medical condition which will have an impact on your chances of conceiving). This is because even if you do everything 'right', you still only have a 25-30 percent chance of conceiving in any given cycle. Try to keep in mind that baby making is a numbers game.

So now you have to go through the waiting, the ovulation plotting, the constant measuring of BBT (Basal body temperatures), tracking periods, and waiting until that magical 5-day window pops up every month, followed by an agonizing wait for Aunt Flo (not) to drop by. For 12. Months. Let me tell you my own from personal experience, that year is quite possibly the most frustrating 12 months you will go through. To give you an idea, it tends to go a little something like this:

Months 1-3

Oh, my goodness, this is so exciting, we are going to have a baby! I should analyse everything and start tracking my periods, not to mention and my ovulation. Should I buy one of those ovulation kits? (goes to boots and buys an expensive ovulation kit, downloads an app for tracking periods and whatnot) While I'm here I should definitely get some pregnancy tests. I mean, it's not going to take long, and they don't expire right (yes, they do expire).

Months 3-6

Ok, we haven't got pregnant yet, but that's ok, these things take time, right? I mean, we don't want one right away do we? It's good to be prepared, to plan, and take our time, I mean, we have so much to consider, a new house, baby names, everything. It's no big deal. Maybe we need to have sex more, because how regular is regular. (Starts looking up "best foods to eat while trying to get pregnant" and other such articles). I haven't even looked up my maternity leave policy - does my work even have one? Oh look, couple X is pregnant, aw, that's nice, that'll be us soon. This is so exciting. Is it too soon to start taking folic acid?

Months 6-9

Seriously, what is wrong with us? I've done everything that those articles told me to do, I'm eating healthy, I'm exercising (Am I exercising too much? Did I manage to dislodge a developing egg while I was out running last week?). I've stopped having my Starbucks every morning, we've cut back on the wine. He's not wearing tight underwear any more, I'm putting little stickers on the calendar to show when my ovulation window is open, hang on a sec, are we having sex enough? What do they mean when they say regular? I still don't know what that means. Do they mean a regular position, or a regular amount? We did it 4 times last month over my ovulation period, am I not making any eggs? Does he have slow swimmers?

Google's more articles on getting pregnant

Tries to confide in friends, bless them, they all try their best but generally they quite often put their foot in it and say something frustrating. Like "It'll happen when it's meant to happen" or "You're obviously trying too hard, you need to stop thinking about it." I know they mean well but it's not helpful in the slightest.

Months 9-12

*Start questioning oneself repeatedly, not to mention my partner. *

WHAT IS WRONG WITH US?! In the last year 3 of our friends have gotten pregnant; why not us? We've done everything right. I can pinpoint my ovulation within a few days tolerance. I've tried everything... I'm considering those herbal treatments now, I hate acupuncture, and I'm exhausted. My partner must be bored of me talking about it - what if he doesn't want to have kids anymore? Worse still, what if he doesn't want to have kids with ME? Tries to confide in mum, who replies with "Well it didn't take me long, I managed to get pregnant pretty. Your sister managed to pop them out fine - are you sure you're doing it often enough?" No, mum, I'm sorry I'm not talking about my sex life with you. Tries to talk to friends, who are probably sick of talking to me about it now, I'm guessing that is why they always change the subject. I'm Feeling a bit down and depressed about all this now, I mean, this is what we are put here to do right? This is our main purpose and I can't fulfil that one thing. What is the point? If I have to make another excuse or story about why we don't have kids, I'm definitely going to cry.

You end up exhausted, emotional, confused, and you don't really know what to do with yourself anymore.

The prospect of facing any kind of infertility is extremely distressing to live with. It's one of those topics many people are of the opinion no-one else really understands what it feels like to have to face this. Your friends, family and work colleagues, no matter how close they are, often can't relate to how you are feeling. It can seem like a very lonely and isolating journey.

"I went to my NHS Dr first & first & they had referred me a local fertility clinic (NHS). We had no clue about any existing problem. Unfortunately, I viewed myself very unfavourably as being 'built wrong' so I always suspected I was doing something wrong. But I never wanted to face what it was and that bad thinking stopped me from finding out if there was a medical problem for far too long.

The fertility clinic saw me 3 months after referral to a bombardment of tests. Other half had one test involving a pot! I had loads - bloods, swabs, operations, drugs... it was relentless.

My first appointment to discuss the initial results with them was the scariest thing ever. I had no clue about what they were going to say. My partner was fine but I had ovulation problems but they weren't sure exactly what the cause was - that set off a ton of other investigations. I heard the first 10 minutes of what the doctor said and then my head went 'problem with me, problem with me.... over & over' until the tears wouldn't stop. But I didn't have a chance to reflect as they needed more tests so I had to walk 10 minutes down the road to give more blood. After I gave my partner a kiss & hug goodbye I walked off - it was raining and I had an umbrella up but it was raining inside my umbrella the entire walk there.
 Then I had a laparoscopic op 2 months later & all was fine - tubes clear & no endometriosis. We were given one month's try on Clomid in an attempt to get the ovulation cycles going but it didn't work, so in January we had to make the biggest decision. They could offer me IVF on the NHS but we were only allowed one try as I was 40 in February the same year and then there was no funding."

I mean, how exhausting does all that sound?

"At first in the early few years when I was in denial & couldn't speak about it everyone seemed not to understand & an enemy. There certainly are quite a lot of insensitive attitudes in our culture anyway. They didn't understand because I couldn't talk about it. I felt they didn't care because it seemed obvious to me that I was struggling. I think I expected too much."

The grief you feel, every single month is without question the hardest thing I've had to come to terms with. Every month is such an emotional roller coaster. Going through the motions of "right, let's be positive," to getting to that precious 5-day window and making the most of it. Then the two weeks of waiting for Aunt Flo to drop by, and the inconsolable feeling of emptiness and hatred when she does.

The money wasted on expensive ovulation and fertility kits, pregnancy tests, and every pill, magazine and internet articles claiming "1001 things that can boost your chances of getting pregnant" just make you feel worthless, because none of them work. (for example, bananas may help with sperm health, but what works for one doesn't work for another. You could eat so many bananas you feel like a banana, but it's very unlikely to have a profound effect). Then, low and behold, a friend, work colleague, or family member announces to the world that they are having a baby - and it took them by surprise, they weren't even planning on it. Just when you think you can't feel any worse!

The best way I can describe this feeling is to imagine that every month you are given the opportunity to earn something you want so badly, to the point that it hurts, and you cherish the idea that this could be the month that you finally get it to then have it taken away from you every month, to then have to tell yourself time and time again, "it's OK, we didn't have it anyway."
You then spend the next week analysing in minute detail what you did wrong that month, did you drink too much coffee? Did the sushi you eat have anything to do with it? Were you too stressed (again, there are dozens of papers that have proven that stress has very little impact)? Did you not do a handstand for long enough after you had sex? And then you find yourself blinking and before you know it, two years have gone by and you've done nothing. Nothing. You've not made the move to a new job, because you don't want to lose your maternity entitlement. You haven't been away on holiday because you're saving for IVF. You haven't moved to a new house. Or you've moved to a new house to be closer to your family and to get ready for family life, but it's not happened. Your life gets put on hold. It's emotionally taxing, not to mention it's psychologically exhausting.

It's such a difficult set of emotions to explain, but the thing is, we do have emotions. We do have feelings, so if you want to cry or vent or scream into a pillow - just do it! No One has the right to tell you not to be upset by it, and before anyone pipes up, no you can't just get over it. The emotional distress you go through is painful, and telling yourself it doesn't matter, and having others tell you it doesn't matter, or to just relax, it'll happen when it happens, doesn't make anything better. It's similar to being told you have a serious illness, without there being an illness. Because you get told "this is the problem. This is what we can do. It might work, it might not, but until we try, we don't know". Although people will always try and offer you a solution, it's not something that can just be fixed. The emotional grief reaction that comes with it can be unbearable. It's frightening. It's traumatising. It can feel so isolating.

If this sounds like something you have experienced, I would just like to say one thing to you;

Although you might feel like it, you are not alone.

Don't believe me? These are real life comments from a handful of women I know, all with different stories.

"At 25 someone I hardly knew said 'oh are you one of those kid haters? What was the point in getting married so young if you're not having kids?'
I literally died. I had to leave work early and cried the whole way home. All I ever wanted was to have children. I'm so glad my little one is here but people don't think that their words can be so hurtful."

"My basic story is that I'm in my early 30's, I have PCOS, and have been told that I'll never get pregnant without medical help (even worse hearing that when I had an early miscarriage at 18). All my friends and family (and a lot of people I meet) ask when I'm going to "settle down and start a family" and I often get told that "the clock is ticking!". Add to this that I work as a nursery nurse and it gets incredibly frustrating sometimes!"

"It took us nearly a year and although that's not a long time compared to some I felt really shocked - people 'accidentally' get pregnant all the time so every month it felt like my body was stick 2 fingers up to me! I Honestly thought that when we said, 'yes we'd like to have a baby now please' it would just happen. I don't think anyone really considers that it might not turn out that way until it happens to them"

"I have recently discovered that I may be 'reproductively challenged'. At 30, I was utterly devastated. Thankfully, my partner is supportive and wonderful, but whenever we want to think about starting to have children, it won't be a 'let's have kids!' type of discussion, and it may take us a very long time. I wish more people would talk about these things, it's more common than we all know. And if we spoke about it more, perhaps we'd feel less isolation."

" I come from Asian descent(Pakistani) so in our culture it's very common for women to conceive right away after the wedding, which we didn't. And no ovulation didn't help much. Every time we would talk to a relative, the imminent question would be, "is there good news on its way?", "are you trying to prevent?", "have you gotten yourself checked?". In our culture, it's inevitably taken as the girl is the one who is defective/barren however you may want to put it. It's incredibly hurtful"

"We have been trying to have a baby for over 3 years and had already both had fertility assessments and were about to go for treatment when I was lucky enough to fall pregnant, again. I also had an early miscarriage and it was one of the most upsetting, soul destroying things ever. Every day of this pregnancy I am checking for blood and praying that I don't find any."

"The main things that bothered me were feelings of guilt and inadequacy. Oh, the guilt! Guilt at not being able to have a normal womanly body that could produce a child for my husband. Guilt that I couldn't produce a child for me. But more than anything, overwhelming, gut-wrenching guilt that I couldn't produce a sibling for my daughter. She used to ask me why she couldn't have a wee baby sister or brother like all her friends and it broke my heart."

"After speaking to my mum's contact, I realised it wasn't just me and that the heart-breaking failure of fertility problems affects lots of people. She explained how she'd always succeeded in life and done well and this was the first time she'd failed (over several months) and felt out of control to fix it. I felt just the same. She helped me think of a small step and told me all about her journey to being a mother of two and a private Dr in Bristol who was fantastic."

There are many different forums, support groups and helplines that you can get in touch with, if you feel like you have no one to turn to. If you are feeling like you don't have anyone to talk to, I would urge you to seek out one of these groups to confide in a professional or a peer group who knows what you are going though. (Heck, if you really want to, you can talk to me, I've got two ears and a lot of time for people who are going through this). Support groups offer the chance to meet up, chat and share experiences with others who are also struggling to conceive. It is a time to share your journey and listen to others experiences, for mutual peer support and also a time to learn from others.

A support group can be informal – taking place in someone's home or in a café or more formal at a fertility clinic with professional guest speakers. Some support groups are ladies only, others for partners too.

We went to a great support group at Southampton Hospital, which was run by a lovely lady called Ruth. She was a senior Councillor at the Complete Fertility Clinic. It was a free meeting that is held once a month, and anyone can go along, regardless of where you are on your journey, or if you're being treated at the clinic.

Going into it, we had no idea what it was going to be like. Was is going to be like a fertility fight club, where the first rule is you don't talk about it outside of the fight club? The opening conversation we all had while waiting for everyone else to arrive was what the men's room is like in a fertility clinic. A few years ago, a photographer Andrew Buurman went around the country and took pictures of all the different men's rooms at different clinics. After having to go through the experience himself, it was his way to show the other side of infertility. It was quite the ice breaker.

There were four couples there, all with different stories and circumstances. One couple had PCOS and a low swimmer count. Another couple were over the age limit for NHS funded fertility treatment and were looking at the options available to them.

Another couple were in a similar situation to us, at the beginning of the journey on the infertility bus, not sure which stop was theirs. We all sat there at the beginning talking about how everything we were going through had made us feel, including how it felt when we spoke to our families and friends. We talked about how frustrating the whole thing is. It was a relief to be able to vent frustrations around friends, family members and other peoples maybe less sensitive approach to our infertility. I guess it was also nice to know that you're not overreacting, it is a big deal, and that there are others who are in the same boat as you. It was sort of a bitter sweet comfort.

While we are about talking about your feeling, there is one person you need to open up to more than anyone else about this. That's right, your right-hand man (or indeed woman), partner in crime. talk to your partner, let them know how you are feeling about things, and get them to open up to you too. You'd be surprised how much they will want to talk about this with you, despite what they might want you to believe (men do have feelings after all).

When it comes to your family and your friends, cut them a little slack, for yours and their sake. Because unless they're in the same boat as you, they probably don't know what you're going through. They won't know what to say, and it can be hard for them to get their heads around too - are there any subjects that are off topic? (Not really, I don't think? Maybe just ask us how we are feeling occasionally?) "Do you mind if I share this photo of my baby?" (Nope, we love baby pictures. We can't wait until we can fill everyone's news feed with a picture of 7 of our latest release).

All we ask is that if we're having a bit of a bad day and want to whine about it don't shut us out. If you let us just vent, and let us have a bitch, we appreciate it. We know it's dull playing the same record over and over. Just don't try and force the conversation away from it if we need a good vent. Many many times I will message my friends on WhatsApp or something and just need to get it off my chest, and they're great, they let me get on with it. If you ask them to listen, providing they are a good friend, and I'm sure you are a pretty good judge of character, they will.

I know it's frustrating when those close to you say things like "you're just over thinking it, it'll happen when it's supposed to happen" and "what will be will be", but they're trying to help. So, don't shut them out, because on your darkest days, when you're feeling low and so utterly shit, they are the people you need to have near you, to talk to, cry with, or just eat a shit load of cake and drink buckets of tea. Your support network is the most important thing you will have in your arsenal.

So, you've waited an entire year now (a whole year. Four seasons. 12 months, you get the picture). For some, this wait can be even longer, because you don't know that it can be a problem. For years, I completely ignored the fact that certain things did or didn't happen, such as not having a period for 6 months, yet not being pregnant at any time. Or feeling incredibly bloated and sick, but not going to the doctors for a check-up, because hey, I was single, and I wasn't having sex, and so I couldn't possibly be pregnant, and who cares? Ill deal with it when I have to.

I was living my life, and I had many other items on the list that were above my reproductive abilities. Things such as getting myself a decent flat, and a car, and looking after my cat, seeing my friends, and all those other things you do when you are single. I'm also a runner, so I was running races at least once a month, and I was training hard for marathons and the like, clocking up to 150 miles in a month sometimes. (It sounds impressive, but it's not, some months I ran about 60. I'm not a natural runner, I run until I'm hungry and then empty my fridge) On occasion my period wouldn't show up, so I put it down to the running because that's a thing that happens. It just wasn't my top priority.

I still can't believe that was my attitude. (This is where the feelings of questioning myself, self-loathing, and utter hatred for my body kick in. I promised that I would keep this light hearted.) But I was young free and single for a long time after someone broke my heart by telling me that having children was so important, and the fact that we hadn't had kids meant I couldn't be worth loving. So, I just tried really really hard to squash those feelings away and forget about it and focus on other things in the meantime. But I'm getting off topic now. Right, back to it.

So. picture the scene. You've decided to go and speak to a medical professional about your desires to have a baby, and you're sat there, in the waiting room, and you don't really know what to expect. Your partner is here, and to be honest, neither of you really know what he's doing here, because surely what he has to go through isn't required until a little later, right?

So, you go into your GPs office, and you sit down and you explain to the doctors your situation, and they sit there calmly and listen to what you say, and tap some notes, and then they look at you and ask some very bog-standard questions along the lines of:

- How long have you been trying for a baby?

- How often do you have sex?

- Do you have any medical conditions that can affect that area?

- Do either of you already have any children?

Answer all the above correctly, and you will be referred to a specialist, and have to book a bunch of tests. These will include blood tests for hormone profiling, which are done on day 21 and day 1-2 of your cycles to make sure you are producing the right hormones and ovulating. You'll also have to have an internal examination to ensure your ovaries and cervix are all good, and for your GP to make sure there are no abnormalities. When I had this done I was told my cervix was inflamed, but it's nothing to really worry about.

Your partner will need to have sperm analysis done too. After all the results have been collated you will be able to sit down with the GP and discuss your options, which will usually result in a referral. (Note - depending on your area, if you already have children, either together or from a previous relationship, you won't eligible for NHS funded treatment). Something I was really shocked to find out, is that you need to make sure that the doctor you are seeing has an interest or some sort of expertise in fertility treatments. This shouldn't really matter, surely? However, if they have an interest or experience in this area, then it is likely that there is more they can do in the way of giving advice and initiating basic investigations. If your doctor has no particular interest in infertility, they should at least be able to refer you to someone who can help you. Many women express their frustrations about the years of disappointment before they have plucked up the courage to see their family doctor.

The "appointments system" deters some patients from "bothering" the doctor over something they think they might regard as being trivial. This will not be helped if you have already experienced another doctor giving you an airy dismissal that everything is sure to be alright and that you have got plenty of time to get pregnant - the "go away and don't worry about it" response. The long and short of it is, from the very first phone call, you have to insist you speak to someone who will actually help you.

I remember going to a smear test earlier this year (ladies, the things we must go through.) and I expressed to the nurse that I wanted to look at exploring the avenue of fertility testing. She looked at me quite blankly for about half a second before turning back to her computer screen and told me "oh, you shouldn't be worrying about that, I mean, not yet. If you've not been trying for a year they won't do anything anyway. It will happen when it happens". It really worries me that health professionals can be so completely insensitive about this stuff. Then when I had a complete breakdown in front of my GP a few months later, there was no compassion or emotion, which if I'm honest, made me feel like I was just wasting her time.

(I should probably note that this conversation took place BEFORE my examination. I don't think there is a single topic of conversation that is appropriate when a stranger is staring at your anatomy equipped with various apparatus while you've got your legs positioned like a frog with your feet in stirrups)

And then the appointment happens right away, right?

Wrong.

Regardless of you going through the NHS or going privately, like most good things, this will take time. And before you start, yes, I know you've already been waiting at least a year, but remember from earlier, when I told you that 3.5 million people in the UK are affected by infertility? It's going to be a bit of a wait. You can be waiting anything up to 6 months for a referral appointment.

So, the appointment date has come about, and you both find yourselves once again, sat in a waiting room, reading 6 months out of date magazines (or, if you're my Mr, playing words with friends and tweeting about NASA) and feeling a bit nervous and not sure what to expect. I mean, do they brand you like cattle with a big INFERTILE stamp? (I doubt it, because that would probably force us to talk about this much more than we do). One of the ladies I spoke to described the fertility unit as being a little like a cattle market, people just herded in and sat around waiting for their number to be called out. (maybe less like a cattle market, more like a cheese counter at the supermarket?)

Your name gets called out.

This is it.

Judgement day. Sort of.

So…. what kind of experience can you expect?

Infertility experts are just that. Experts. So, they are going to ask you questions about your sexual history and you should not be afraid to explain it to them, they will have heard every story you can think of. Also, don't try and cut them any crap, because it'll just make things worse. Also, they will have your medical notes. Ladies, it will be beneficial to come equipped with all the information you have on your periods (how regular, how long they last, are they painful - that period tracker app data will all be worth it, I promise!). Because any abnormalities will need to be addressed. Plus, you will be asked how long you have been off the pill or any other form of contraceptive for, and any problems you might have had with it. If you have children from a previous relationship, you will be asked to divulge in information surrounding your ex partner's fertility.

Once you've gotten to know one another on a much more personal level than one does with strangers, you will likely go through several tests, including:

- **Blood tests** *(Him and Her, to check your hormone levels are tip top. This is particularly important for women, as lower hormone levels, combined with sporadic or absence altogether of periods is a sign of PCOS. A Drop-in testosterone can also lead to sperm problems.)*

- **Sperm analysis** *- your male companion will be asked for a, ahem, contribution, which they will check to ensure that his little swimmers are healthy. They check they are swimming in the right direction, and can swim fast enough (No One likes lazy swimmers). If for any reason, he is firing blanks, further investigative tests, including surgery may be required. This will attend to any blockages or other problems that may arise.*

- **STD tests** *- Chlamydia is the most common STI in the UK. You can have it, and for months not even know. It can cause pelvic inflammatory disease and fertility problems. It can cause cysts the size of lemons to form on your ovaries and your womb, which you don't know about for almost a year. It can cause the most intense pains, and every time you go to your doctor, they will brush it off as IBS, Crohn's disease, or something else.*

They will send you away without even doing an examination or a simple test. It can push your body to breaking point until one day, you find yourself unable to move from the bathroom floor, throwing up constantly, and having to beg one of your family friends to take you to the hospital because you don't want to call an ambulance, fearing you might be wasting their time. You can then get referred immediately to hospital, where you are nil by mouth and spend 3 weeks in hospital with doctors unable to find out what's wrong, because your doctor didn't do a test. You'll end up having every test and investigative procedure done for stomach conditions, which all return inconclusive. You can have investigative surgery for a bowel condition, only to wake up after 7 hours of surgery with a huge scar on your stomach and a tube coming out of your side draining off poisonous fluid. It can almost kill you. You spend another 3 weeks in hospital recovering, and just when you are leaving the hospital, someone will tell you that you might not be able to have children, but to just pop back to the doctors when that time comes. Tell me, How the fuck am I supposed to take on all of this when I'm 18 years old?

(I said I wouldn't go into detail, but that's as much as I can give you right now without bursting into tears. Game face Hollie. Man up.)

You can buy a test over the counter at most pharmacies these days. As someone who completely lost faith in her family doctor after the way my diagnosis was mishandled I would urge you to do this. It costs about £12 and could save your life. If you get nothing else from this book please do this. This goes for men and women. Your GP can also perform this test. The consequences of not doing it can be fatal and cause you years of confusion, agony, heartache and feeling like you are worth nothing. So please, do the damn test.

- **Ultrasound scan** - these will make sure all your plumbing is working correctly. They will check the woman's ovaries, womb and fallopian tubes. In a transvaginal ultrasound scan, which takes place in hospital, a small ultrasound probe is used, and helps doctors check the health of your ovaries and womb.

Certain conditions that can affect the womb, such as endometriosis and fibroids, can prevent pregnancy from happening. The scan can also check for blockages in your fallopian tubes, which may be stopping eggs from travelling along the tubes and into the womb, which can result in an ectopic pregnancy.

Depending on the outcome of this, you may have to go for surgery. Please note, that if this happens, it's not the be all and end all.

"It was during this laparoscopy that endometriosis was discovered and diagnosed. Apparently, the extent of my scarring or adhesions was reasonably severe, and was causing kinks and squashes in my Fallopian tubes. An attempt was made to release some of the bands of scarring, but trying to do so without causing additional scarring can be tricky. I had a strange sense of relief on the diagnosis of this condition. My years (5 years and counting at that point) of heavy bleeding and crippling pain made a lot more sense. I wasn't imagining it all!"

- **X-ray of fallopian tubes** - *Otherwise called a hysterosalpingogram (HSG). Opaque dye is injected through the cervix while you have an X-ray. The dye will help your doctors to see if there are any blockages in your fallopian tubes.*

So, once you've had all these tests done, it'll be quick to get the result back, right?

Nope, wrong again.

You'll need to wait for a couple of weeks at the least to find out the results of your tests. When the call finally comes and you have to go back, these tests will uncover a cause in around just 80% of the time. In the remaining 20% of cases, no clear cause can be found, aka unexplained infertility. Whether or not a clear cause is found, your GP can talk you through the next steps. This may include referral to a fertility clinic for further investigation or treatment.

OH MY GOD ANOTHER APPOINTMENT.

Yep, I'm afraid so. This can be going one of two ways:

If your doctor has found a root cause to your problems, you will discuss with them what to do next, and what options for treatment you have. This may involve surgery, it may involve a round of tablets or injections, this will all depend on your personal circumstances.

If your tests have returned inconclusive, be prepared to have to go through more testing, and potentially investigative surgery (Repeat as necessary).

Whatever happens at this stage, it may result in IUI (that's intrauterine Insemination), or IVF. (In-Vitro-Fertilisation). If you get to this stage and you are presented with this, I personally cannot explain what going through all the above testing and frustration is like. So rather than fluff it up and tell you it will all go swimmingly, which it won't, one of my lovely ladies (Let's call her L) explained this all to me perfectly:

"Once I'd recovered from that operation (for endometriosis), the consultant in charge of fertility let me try a course of Clomid, to see if that might do the trick. His parting words were "If you're not pregnant after a year, you probably won't conceive naturally". I left his office assuming that he felt hopeful I would in fact fall pregnant. I naively had high hopes that it would be enough, as it seems to work for many women. It wasn't, and it didn't.

In 2014 I had my second laparoscopy. I vividly remember getting home to a letter on the doormat giving me a date for my next operation, then my phone ringing. It was my younger sister calling to excitedly tell me she was expecting her first child. The first grandchild. I hoped I'd made all the right excited noises, and said all the right things. I hung up, and sobbed for an hour in the shower.

Trying to explain the paradox to someone who just doesn't understand is difficult. To be incredibly, genuinely happy and excited for other people who are expecting a child, but desperately sad and jealous for yourself simultaneously is a conundrum. In the few years of operations and longing I went through before even speaking to a fertility clinic, my sister and her husband had my gorgeous niece, my brother and his wife had my precious nephew, and my husband's sister had our two wonderful nephews on that side of our family too.

I love being an auntie. I'm pretty darn good at it too. I have earned a name for myself for giving the best gifts, doing the most spoiling, and arguably being great at giving some getting-to-sleep snuggles when they were small too. The joy I experience from seeing these lovely little humans growing and learning makes me wish that I had my very own to love and teach and parent, and not have to give back, and there are scores of aunties and uncles and honorary godparents worldwide who feel the same.

It was following this second procedure that the consultant's parting words were "I'll have to sign you off my books. There's nothing more I can do for you". On this occasion, I left his office and cried all the way down the corridor, through the waiting room and out of the hospital. Crying in public is not something I do lightly."

The whole process of going through all the testing, the blood tests, the prodding, poking, the ultrasounds, can wear you down. It can feel never ending and like you're getting nowhere. One thing that the community I have spoken to about this, is a common theme of "I wish people spoke about this more. I felt so isolated and alone, not feeling like I can talk to anyone about how this is making me feel. I'm exhausted, I'm emotional, I'm stressed out, and I'm stuck in this bubble with no way out".

The important thing here is, you are not alone. You are not in a bubble on your own. There are 3.5 million people around the UK who are in the same bubble as you. I promise you, that there are people out there that you can talk to. If you don't want to speak to a health professional (and to be honest I completely get that, sometimes you don't want facts, you just want someone to listen) then I can only urge you to look up and seek out a support group in your local area. I know, I know, I'm repeating myself, but if you don't feel you can confide in friends and family, these groups are a fantastic respite for couples in our position, if nothing else, to help you to realize and understand that you're not going crazy and you're not overreacting. It might feel weird, but these communities really are amazing at being just a place for you to vent and listen to others who are going through the same thing as you.

It doesn't have to be a physical support group either - I have a period tracker app installed on my phone which has a social area, with many many forums where women in a similar situation will vent their frustrations, talk about their appointments, success stories, the not so successful stories, share their POAS (that's Pee on a Stick) photos, their charts, everything, it is incredibly comforting to know that even when you are feeling so isolated, there are other women out there who will support you, and offer you words of support, sympathy and encouragement. If I'm going to repeat myself it will be with this - YOU ARE NOT ALONE.

Act Three - PCOS, Endometriosis and other Blockages

So, let's talk about the three main reasons why women are infertile. For this chapter, I have two lovely ladies who have kindly shared their stories about the impact the above has had on their struggles, and along with this, I guess I'll have to open up about my own problems (especially after that outburst in Act 2, right?)

From all the women I have spoken to, PCOS (Poly cystic ovary syndrome) and Endometriosis seem to be the top of the pile when it comes to primary infertility causes in women. Shall we get some science on these first? Yes, I think we should.

PCOS - Polycystic Ovary Syndrome.

"So, I hadn't had a period in about 5 months, wasn't pregnant, so I went to the doctors who gave me a blood test. They phoned me on Christmas eve (wonderful timing) to let me know that my bloods had shown a chemical / hormonal imbalance linked with PCOS. Meaning that my body doesn't ovulate frequently. Brief explanation over the phone, and then booked in for a follow up appointment in the new year. I cried a lot."

So, what is PCOS?

Polycystic ovary syndrome is described by the NHS as a common condition that affects how a woman's ovaries work. There are three main conditions of PCOS:

- **Irregular periods** – which means your ovaries don't regularly release eggs,

- **Excess androgen** – higher than normal levels of "male hormones" in your body, which can cause a number of physical signs such as excess facial or body hair and weight gain

- **Polycystic ovaries** – *this is when your ovaries become enlarged and contain many fluid-filled sacs (otherwise known as follicles) which surround the eggs. it's worth noting that, despite its nasty name, if you have PCOS you don't actually have cysts at all.*

So how do you know if you've got PCOS? Well, as you can tell by what C said when I asked her to open up about her experiences, she didn't even know she had PCOS until last Christmas.

"I read an article on someone who at 30 had decided to come off the pill after being on it since her teens - like myself. And it had cleared up loads of different ailments she had been suffering with. One of which was IBS - also to note I had already had various different scans and tests for stomach issues, including an ultrasound, and a blood test for coeliac as my dad suffers from it and they had just put it down to 'IBS'.... they hadn't picked up on anything else 'wrong' with me. Terrible really when you think about it...."

This reduced me to tears. When I read that another woman had been let down so badly by her GP, due to a misdiagnosis, it just breaks my heart. Which is why it is so so important for women who have any worry or feel like things with their periods aren't normal at all should go to their doctor sooner rather than later. I don't care if your 18, 28, or 48, if you feel like something is not right down there, go and see a doctor, and if you are not happy with your result from them, you have every right to go back and ask for a second opinion. I had to go to the doctor around 14 times over the space of 12 months and still was not diagnosed with anything until it was too late. Anyway, more of that later. Back to this chapter first. The main signs of PCOS are:

- *Irregular periods or no periods at all*
- *Excessive hair growth, usually on the face, chest, back or butt*
- *Weight gain*
- *Thinning hair and hair loss from the head*
- *Oily skin or acne.*

PCOS affects around 1 in 10 women around the UK, and is hereditary. Therefore, if you know it runs in your family (Yup, you're gonna have to talk about this with your nearest and dearest) it's worth going to your doctor and discussing this, especially if your periods are irregular or non-existent.

If you do have PCOS, it is not the end of the world. I have spoken to a couple of women who have been diagnosed with PCOS and have gone on to have children with treatment. If you are in this situation, I'm going to be honest with you, it's not going to be easy, and it will be a long-winded process. You will probably have to have some sort of medical intervention, whether that be with surgery to remove follicles, or full on IUI or more likely IVF. The infertility rate with polycystic ovaries is very high. Some women with polycystic ovary syndrome will ovulate every now and again - others might never ovulate. Because the condition is quite complex and can go un-diagnosed for so long, it is difficult to spot. Without doing a serious amount of ovulation tests to see when you are ovulating, and even then, it won't be consistent, it may be months between ovulation cycles. Therefore, women with PCOS tend to require IVF in order to have children.

"I wasn't even sure if / when I wanted to have children, so to be told that I might find it difficult was a bit of a headfuck (for want of a better way of putting it). Being forced to think about something that I'm not ready for, and not sure if I even want is weird. It's made us think that if I were to 'accidentally' get pregnant, it would be a completely different attitude now. I had a long chat with my mum about it, and then another friend who suffers from a similar situation. What I didn't realize was how common it was. I even spoke to my boss because I was having so many appointments. She asked, in a nice way, if everything was OK because I kept taking time for medical things. So, I told her, and then she told me that she also has a similar condition / imbalance. It was nice to speak to someone who has been there, done it, and come out the other side. She has a son who is 6 now, and it gave me a bit of comfort."

Let's have a look at Endometriosis.

"After spending several years trying and failing to fall pregnant the romantic way with my husband, we realized something was awry. Perhaps I always had a niggling feeling it wouldn't be easy, or at least there may be something wrong with me.

 After discussing the number of years we'd been trying to conceive with my doctor, I was referred to hospital for some investigative surgery.

 It was during this laparoscopy that endometriosis was discovered and diagnosed. Apparently, the extent of my scarring or adhesions was reasonably severe, and was causing kinks and squashes in my Fallopian tubes. An attempt was made to release some of the bands of scarring, but trying to do so without causing additional scarring can be tricky"

I contacted Endometriosis UK for the information on this topic combined with personal accounts from some of the ladies I've spoken to.

Endometriosis (pronounced en- doh – mee – tree – oh – sis) is a condition where cells like the ones in the lining of the womb are found elsewhere in the body. Each month these cells react in the same way as those in the womb, building up and then breaking down and bleeding. But unlike the cells in the womb that leave the body as a period, this blood has no way to escape. This can cause inflammation, pain and the formation of scar tissue.

It is a chronic and debilitating condition that causes extremely painful or heavy periods, and may also lead to infertility, chronic fatigue and bowel and bladder problems. Around 1.5 million women in the UK are currently living with the condition.

- *1 in 10 women of reproductive age in the UK suffer from endometriosis, around 1.5 million women.*
- *10% of women worldwide have endometriosis - that's 176 million worldwide.*

- The prevalence of endometriosis in women with infertility be as high as to 30–50%.
- Endometriosis is the second most common gynaecological condition in the UK.
- On average, it takes 7.5 years from onset of symptoms to get a diagnosis.

The cause of endometriosis is unknown and there is no definite cure.

There are treatments available for endometriosis. They are in the form of surgery, hormone treatments and pain relief, and it does not necessarily mean you cannot have children, again, it's going to take a little bit of time. L's story really touched me when she spoke about how she felt when she was finally given her diagnoses, but the doctor didn't seem to really approach the subject after this, and she was just prescribed clomid and sent on her way.

"Once I'd recovered from that operation, the consultant in charge of fertility let me try a course of Clomid, to see if that might do the trick. His parting words were "If you're not pregnant after a year, you probably won't conceive naturally". I left his office assuming that he felt hopeful I would in fact fall pregnant. I naively had high hopes that it would be enough, as it seems to work for many women. It wasn't, and it didn't.

It was following this (second procedure for endometriosis) that the consultant's parting words were "I'll have to sign you off my books. There's nothing more I can do for you". On this occasion, I left his office and cried all the way down the corridor, through the waiting room and out of the hospital. Crying in public is not something I do lightly. "

L is a testament to women who never give up. After being told that there was nothing more the consultant could do to help her, she did as many couples do and sought private help in the form of IVF.

"After realizing that the only way we'd have any chance of attempting a pregnancy was going to be via IVF, the world became a pretty difficult place for a while. At this point we knew any NHS funding would not be available to us due to the criteria set in our area. We could tick every box, except the one which asks, "do you or your partner have any children?"

My husband's two boys, despite not living with us, meant that we - even though the fertility issue was mine - would not receive any financial help towards treatment. They are lovely boys, but they're not my children, and I suppose due to their ages, we've never had stepparent/stepchildren relationships.

I became quite depressed throughout this period. I saw babies everywhere. Everyone, or so it seemed, was posting their obligatory 12-week scan shots online. I was unhelpfully told "Try to focus on something else. You can't put your life on hold". But my life WAS on hold. I always imagined I'd have children. I'd done my work experience as a 14-year-old in the crèche of the junior school my mother taught in and loved it. I loved being surrounded by these innocent, inquisitive faces who thought I was the bee's knees for drawing cartoon aliens, or expertly gluing wool to card to make a horse's mane.

I joked sarcastically that I'd keep an immaculate, child unfriendly house (I don't). That we'd hire a muscle car and drive across America being young, carefree and, OK, not single, but you know, enjoying our crazy, rich existence (we haven't).

That's the thing about being on an infertility rollercoaster. Life continues. Other people fall pregnant. You still have to go to work, even if you've spent the night crying and disappointed again because your period has arrived. Your best friends, sisters, colleagues, and the entire universe still fall pregnant, sometimes at the drop of a hat (or pants). You don't suddenly have lots more disposable income to take frivolous holidays. All that happens is you take a holiday which some parented-up friends jealously say "I wish we could go to Spain. We're off to Butlins again because little Jemima gets plane sick."

Or your sibling makes a snide remark about your immaculate white blouse and wide-awake eyes "I can't wear white, I'm constantly covered in baby food. I wish I looked as well rested as you, I've been up all night with so-and-so".

In more diplomatic moments you manage to smile, and retort with an "Aren't I lucky". In less diplomatic moments, as my sister discovered, she'd receive an earful of "I WISH I had a child to keep me up all night, you ungrateful f---"; You get the idea. "

Going back to act one, it is so important to remember that the sympathy works both ways when you are on the infertility train. And what L says here is so true. Life does go on. The world does not stop just because you can't have children. You will see others around you who are going through the pregnancy cycle and you know what? It's OK to cry and feel like shit and to be jealous and to wish you could be in their shoes. You cannot bottle these feelings up. You're a human being, and grieving is something that you are allowed to do. Because if not, there will be one day when all that emotion, the hatred, the feeling like shit, the worthlessness and the jealousy will eat you up and you will explode (trust me, I know).

On the flip side, if you do snap at someone, don't forget to apologize. This is going to be a long ass journey and the last thing you want to do is alienate yourself to the world, especially your friends and family. I have confided in my older sister and my friends many times over the last few years about my situation and even though sometimes I want to scream because another friend has just had a baby or announced they're expecting a baby, you can't let this consume you. Be happy for them, because when it happens to you, they will be insanely happy.

L is now a mum to the most scrummy little boy, and she truly is an incredible and inspiring woman.

And then there's me. I kind of already explained what my cause of infertility was, which is PID, or Pelvic Inflammatory Disease.

So, you probably want to know some facts about PID. In my 11 years since I left the hospital, I have read up on this many times, more so in the last 3 years or so. Off the top of my head, and with a little help from the Fertility Network, here are some fun filled facts about PID:

Pelvic inflammatory disease (PID) is an infection of the female upper genital tract, including the womb, fallopian tubes and ovaries. It's estimated that around 1 in 10 women with PID becomes infertile because of the condition.

PID is a common condition, although it's not clear how many women are affected in the UK. Mainly because it can go undetected for so long, and is rather difficult to diagnose, hence why it is dubbed "the silent killer". The worst thing about PID, is that because it doesn't have any visible symptoms until it's too late, women have mild symptoms that may include one or more of the following:

- *Pain around the pelvis or lower abdomen*
- *Discomfort or pain during sex that's felt deep inside the pelvis*
- *Pain during urination*
- *Bleeding between periods and after sex*
- *Heavy periods, painful periods*
- *Unusual vaginal discharge, especially if it's yellow or green*

Most cases of PID are caused by a bacterial infection that's spread from the vagina or the cervix to the reproductive organs higher up. In about one in four cases, it's caused by a sexually transmitted infection (STI) such as chlamydia or gonorrhoea. In many other cases, it's caused by bacteria that normally live in the vagina.

If you have any of these symptoms, PLEASE, GO TO YOUR GP.

Delaying treatment for PID or having repeated episodes of PID can increase your risk of serious and long-term complications. Pains such as severe lower abdominal pain, a high temperature and vomiting, along with any of the above should be ringing alarm bells. PLEASE, go to see your doctor., and get to A&E.

There's no simple test to diagnose PID, but you can buy a kit for testing of Chlamydia, which is one of the biggest causes of PID. You can do this in the comfort of your own home, or at the doctors. This way you are eliminating your chances of it developing into PID. Diagnosis is based on your symptoms and the finding of tenderness, via an internal examination. Swabs will be taken from your vagina and cervix, but negative swabs don't rule out PID. I know. Headfuck much.

The good news is, if diagnosed at an early stage, PID can be treated with a course of antibiotics, which usually lasts for 14 days. You'll be given a mixture of antibiotics to cover the most likely infections, and often an injection as well as tablets.
If like me, you don't get a test done by your GP, and it goes unnoticed for over 12 months, the consequences can be fatal at the worst, or at the best, you can be infertile.

"In my case, as I touched on previously, I went back to my doctor around 14 times in a 12-month period with severe stomach pains and incredibly painful periods and period type cramps. It would come and go with some days walking and laughing would feel like someone was kicking me in the stomach and I would be stuck in bed all day, other times I would be completely fine and would have no pain at all. Every time I went to the doctor I was given medication for IBS, Crohn's, trapped wind, everything except what was wrong with me, because no one knew what was wrong. I cannot stress enough how important it is, to get a second opinion if you are not happy with your diagnosis from your GP.

So, one day, my parents were going off to see my older sister, who had had another little baby down in Devon. I had declined to go as I wasn't feeling well. Saturday, I stayed in bed most of the day. Sunday, I woke up early feeling like my insides had been shredded. The morning was spent in bed until around 11am, which was when I started throwing up. I called my mums friend, who wasn't at home, and couldn't take me to the hospital. It crossed my mind to call an ambulance, but I didn't because I didn't want to waste their time.

As an asthmatic, I felt ambulances should be for people who are in real trouble and not someone who is just in a little pain and being sick. I eventually called another of my mum's friends who did take me to the hospital. I was given an examination and then admitted to hospital with a suspected case of appendicitis, but when they did the tests (ultrasound etc) they couldn't see anything wrong with it. Everyone was baffled. I was hungry, tired, scared and confused, and just wanted the nightmare to be over. (I'm not exaggerating, anyone who has been nil by mouth knows how shit it is).

So, the next 2 weeks were spent nil by mouth virtually the whole time, and I had a number of tests done, scans, dye injections, you name it, they did it. And I mean EVERYTHING. Friends and family came to visit, and that made things easier, but the doctors still had no clue what was wrong. Eventually I had to be admitted for surgery because I was in an unreal amount of pain and they couldn't figure out what was up down there. Apparently, I was on the table for 8 hours, and the following day (you'll have to forgive me as I don't really remember much) I remember coming to and having a huge tube coming out of my side and a massive stitch down my stomach, right under my belly button.

I was horrified, and just cried until I hyperventilated. I remained on morphine for a couple of days and was completely incoherent. Friends who came to see me told me I could barely string together a sentence. When I came off the pain relief and had the stitch removed around a week later, I was told I could go home. It was at this point I was told the extent of the damage. They had opened me up with the intention of it being a bowel problem, to find a cyst the size of a lemon on one of my ovaries, which had burst, causing the poison inside to leak into my womb and tubes. I also had a lot of scarring from the PID, and they had to remove an ovary, and part of my bowel. They told me I would likely have problems having children, but when I do want to, just to (and I quote) "pop back in and see us". I honestly didn't give that much thought to it. "

That was when I was 18. I'm not telling you this to be dramatic or for it to be a sob story, and I didn't ever really want to write this, but it's important to know about. And I think as we've gotten to know each other well now, so you deserve to know the honest truth. PID almost killed me.

As the years went on, I read into it every now and again, and I was shocked and disgusted that I hadn't been told the extent of the problem. It wasn't until I was about 24, in a previous relationship where I suffered with an ectopic pregnancy at 11 weeks (a pregnancy in the fallopian tubes instead of the womb), that I really read up on it. It was really fucking scary, and it made me hate my family GP even more for the damage it had caused me when it could have so easily been sorted with tablets for 14 days.

Throughout the last few years, I have battled with how this condition has made me feel. I have had one ectopic pregnancy and a chemical pregnancy at 6 weeks, suffered with depression, anxiety, I attempted suicide at one point because felt so alone. I felt worthless. What on earth could I offer someone in a relationship if I couldn't give them children.

I found it quite difficult to discuss with partners, and would just not tell them until I felt secure that they wouldn't judge me for it. Guess what though? they do, and they did. And guess what? That made me feel even more shit. It's a horrid cycle, one that I went through for a number of years. I sought comfort and help finally in 2012, and went to counselling. On the back of that, I came out of a toxic relationship, and to heal myself, I took myself out of the relationship game for 3 years by choice before I met my Mr in 2015.

Since we have been together I have had 1 chemical pregnancy at 5 weeks. It's tough. I'm not going to lie. I have cried many many times over my fucked-up body, sobbed into my pillow every time I've got my period, felt a pang of jealousy every time I see a friend announcing that they are pregnant. I cursed myself so many times about not insisting on more from my GP. If she had done the tests, who knows, I probably wouldn't be writing this book and telling you all about this. I guess that's the one good thing that has come from this whole experience, I now get to tell you all about this, and once again reiterate that we are not alone in our situation and although you may feel like you will never have children, that there is hope.

There are of course, a number of other reasons why women are infertile, such as:

- *Ovulation problems, which can be caused by a number of factors, such as hormonal imbalance, stress and other lifestyle factors (such as smoking, drinking, drugs etc.) and continual use of the pill with no breaks over several years.*

- *Poor egg quality, which is usually linked to the above, and/or menopause. The older we get; the quality of our egg reserves drops. Those women who go through premature menopause will then have a less bountiful batch of eggs.*

- *Uterine Contour, this was quite complex to look up, but the best description I have found is where the top of your cervix is separated from the neck of the womb. It is also known as a congenital malformation of uterus. Unfortunately, there doesn't seem to be a whole load of information on this. And I wish there was. Because the lady I spoke to who suffered from it (and had her baby through IVF) had little to no information on the subject.*

- *Uterine Fibroids, these are noncancerous tumours that form inside the uterus. Uterine fibroids can cause symptoms in some cases, depending on their size and location, these tend to be a genetic thing. They can contribute towards infertility (how very generous) and are found in 5% to 10% of infertile women*

- *Primary Ovarian Insufficiency (POI), when a woman's ovaries stop producing hormones and producing eggs at a young age. Women with POI don't ovulate regularly, or sometimes not at all, and may have abnormal levels of hormones.*

- *Polyps, another type of noncancerous growth found on the inside of the uterus. Polyps can interfere with the function of the uterus and make it difficult for a woman to remain pregnant after conception. Surgical removal of the polyps can increase the chances for a woman to get pregnant.*

- *Autoimmune Disorders, these cause the body's immune system to attack normal body tissues it would normally ignore. Autoimmune disorders, such as lupus or rheumatoid arthritis, may cause a woman's immune system to reject the egg and prevent it from implanting or cut off the blood supply to an implanted embryo. They may also attack sperm or the reproductive organs. Yikes.*

Seriously ladies, our bodies go through so much shit, and we still manage to pull ourselves out of the dark and carry on going. I want to take this moment right here to tell you, regardless of how you feel right now, to take a look at yourself. Your body is a powerhouse. It goes through so much every single day and is capable of more than you will ever imagine. If you are worried about anything at all, or if any of the above has made you think "Hmmm, my periods are a bit out of whack" or "I'm sure my mum said something about something hormonal or another". Or if you just want peace of mind that your tubes and womb and bells and whistles are all hunky dory, no harm will come to you if you go and see your doctor for a check-up.
You are a goddess and your body is a damn temple. It's also the only one you have. So, cherish it, nourish it, and look after it!

Act Four - Infertility and men - it's not all about the ladies

"When we were trying to conceive, at first, it was great fun. We were having sex often, just as young couples do, but then time wore on and nothing was happening. That was when an app was suggested. Pee sticks were used daily and double-checked with the app to make sure everything was accurate and that would give us the best chance of a pregnancy. We would track cycles and we'd then know when she was most fertile, when we had our best chance that month. With me working offshore, I wasn't always home for "flower time" - the app symbol was a full flower for the best day and the flower had less petals for the less fertile days surrounding it. This meant we obviously missed some months but when I was home, sex seemed to be limited to the flowering days. It started to feel all a little bit robotic, the romantic, fun and spontaneous act of sex had been taken away. It was there to serve as the baby-making process and nothing else. Well, that's how I felt anyway. The fun had been taken out of it. It made things worse. The spontaneity had been taken out of what is meant to be a fun and spontaneous time. The Russian Roulette of will it/won't it be this time had been removed. It was serious business now. A baby was required in my wife's tummy and it was required yesterday."

So, I thought this would be rather an important part to write into this book. Although I wanted to write this from a woman's point of view (because I am one, duh), it's important to remember that men are affected by the infertility struggle too!

I've only spoken with three men who have wanted to open up about that it's like. I guess you guys aren't as comfortable talking to a stranger about what's up down there. So, although this may be a shorter chapter than others, I think it is just as important to write about.

Male infertility can be put into two camps quite simply. It is usually a problem with either the production of swimmers (sorry, Sperm just sounds a bit too clinical for me), or getting them moving. They are not mutually exclusive however, and some men have problems with both a low count and lazy swimmers. They're not usually a hereditary thing, although they have in the past been linked to genetics. But they are most likely going to be due to lifestyle choices and/or environmental factors.

It's quite an even divide between male and female infertility in the UK, of the couples having IVF treatment, 50% will be due to male infertility and 50% due to female infertility. While most of the problems can be identified, up to 20% of infertility in IVF patients has no obvious cause and this can make it much more difficult to treat.

Top tips to keep your little guys happy:

Saunas and hot tubs are trouble
While many men like to follow their workout with a relaxing hot tub or sauna session, if you're trying for a baby it's usually best to keep these to a minimum. Exposure to the high temperatures in saunas and hot tubs can heat things up down there, and if the temperature gets too high, it can kill sperm and interfere with their production. This will end up resulting in low sperm count and motility. The damage isn't permanent, though, so you can go back to the regular routine as soon as you see a positive on that pregnancy test.

Laptops can burn more than just his lap
Considering laptops can get hot enough to burn legs, you guys might want to keep them away from the crown jewels too. There's evidence that like in hot tubs and saunas, the heat from a laptop can raise scrotal temperature, which, again, may interfere with sperm production. While not all experts agree that laptops can cause infertility, if you're trying to conceive, you may want to keep the laptop on a table or desk just to be safe.

Age is a factor
Women are constantly being warned about the difficulty of conceiving as they get older. It turns out that even though men can (and regularly do) father children later in life, male fertility declines with age.

High levels of continuous stress play a major role in fertility

While you might not be surprised that your lifestyle plays a role in fertility, you might not realize how large a role stress can have in both male and female fertility problems. For guys, stress can lead to impotence, erectile dysfunction and even shut down the hypothalamic-pituitary-testicular axis (a fancy term for the group of glands that play a critical role in developing and regulating your reproductive system) — all of which can interfere with fertility. While it's next to impossible to avoid stress completely, it's important for both of you to work on managing your stress, especially if you're finding this whole getting pregnant thing...well, pretty damn stressful. So regularly do stress-reducing activities together, like going for walks, exercising, or just sharing some laughs. Mr and I love going for a long walk, eating some good food, walking alpacas..... Anything that keeps ourselves busy!

Keeping fit and healthy keeps his swimmers fit and healthy

Both of you should watch your weight when you are trying for a baby. Besides it being great for you and your physical and emotional wellbeing, adopting a healthy lifestyle will boost your chances of conceiving. Plus, obesity in men is associated with decreased sperm count and quality. Not to mention excessive weight may also be associated with misshapen sperm, which can interfere with the sperm's ability to reach and penetrate the egg.

The good thing about this, is that more often than not (unless he's firing complete blanks) there are things that can be done to help your fellas little fellas. These can be very simple lifestyle changes, such as not smoking, cutting back on drinking, maintaining a healthy weight, wearing loose fitting underwear and staying away from tight clothing. Keeping the goods cool is important for healthy production.

If you have been referred to a fertility specialist, they will ask for a donation from your partner to conduct sperm analysis. Guys, don't feel weird about this when the nurse hands you a cup and leads you to a room, you're not the first guy who's looked at that plastic beaker and thought "how much do they need?!" and you won't be the last.

Ideally, try to abstain from any bedroom activity the night before. This is where they will check the little guys for their numbers (less than 15 million per ml is considered a low count). Their mobility is checked, ensuring they have been formed correctly and that they are swimming in the right direction (note that if they're going around in circles this is a bad thing, remember that episode of the Simpsons when they see all the little homers swimming into one another - how did they manage to have three kids?). They're programmed to swim in a forward formation. The more that go around in circles, the harder it will be for you to get pregnant. Once this has all been analysed, they can categorize patients into groups, which come with some rather interesting names...

- **Aspermia** - no semen
- **Azoospermia** - semen containing no sperm
- **Oligozoospermia or oligospermia** - sperm concentration is low, less than 15 million per ml
- **Asthenozoospermia or asthenospermia** - less than 40% of the sperm are moving, and less than 32% are swimming progressively
- **Teratozoospermia** – less than 4% of the sperm are normally shaped
- **Oligoasthenoteratozoospermia** (sometimes referred to as OATS, understandably) – less than 15 million sperm per ml with less than 40% being motile and less than 4% are normally shaped
- **Necrospermia** - all sperm are dead
- **Poor viability** - less than 58% are alive
- **Pyospermia or leucospermia** - presence of large number of white blood cells (more than one million/mL) in the semen, often associated with an infection

Once this has been identified, then your fertility specialist can discuss with you the way to work around this. Note there is no cure for male infertility, but you can work with it. IVF and IUI are the best causes of action for this, because they can take a sample (you're gonna get well acquainted with that beaker) "wash" it all clean and pick the strongest swimmers to either directly put inside your partner's cervix, or mix with eggs outside the womb and then implant back in.

So, what's it like, being sat in that office with your beloved, to be told by your GP "We've got your results, and it's you. You have a low sperm count"?

Obviously, I can't comment on how my partner feels about this as yet, because we haven't gone through it. But when we do, I'll let you know. In the meantime, I have spoken to three gentlemen who have been in that chair, and this is what they have told me:

1 – "Not long after my 30th birthday me and my wife, not getting any younger (33 at the time), decided on a trip to the doctors. We'd been trying for about 2 years by this point. We got married on February 8th, 2014 and as to avoid my wife-to-be being "fat" on our wedding day plus the label of having a bastard child, we conscientiously waited until nearer the time before proactively trying for our first child.

We were referred to the fertility clinic who checked us over and eventually the dreaded news came...I was practically infertile. Normal sperm count is considered to be anywhere from 15 million upwards. I had 2.5million! Factors to then consider include missing the target, motility and morphology as to how fertile a man is in terms of percent. If you take away the negating factors, that still only left me/us with a maximum chance of pregnancy of 4% - I'm practically a write-off as far as being a baby making machine goes. No wonder there were no accidents in my younger years. I could sew all I wanted and nothing would ever grow.

I'm a very positive, happy-go-lucky person normally but when I got the news, I hit rock bottom. Sitting there next to my wife, I just wanted the world to swallow me up. I wanted to go home, shut the curtains, grab my dog and go to bed. I wanted to lie in a darkened room, hugging my dog and fall asleep sobbing my little heart out. My spark had gone and life just drained from my body. Instead, I had to hold it together while she cried her eyes out. I didn't know what to do. I was numb.

I've never been medically diagnosed with depression or anxiety, and I don't think I ever would, but I think over this last year it's the closest I've come to it. It's affected me in ways I never thought possible. Just randomly crying at anything and everything baby-related, baby rage, jealousy. Always having that nagging feeling that I might not be able to contribute to what we've always wanted.

Growing up loving football, you always see them with their kids on the pitch celebrating the league or cup win and they always look so young. I thought back then, "I'm going to be a young dad one day. I'm going to be like Beckham et al." Beckham had Brooklyn at 23 and I thought I might follow a similar path. Now I know why I didn't.

One of my best friends now has two kids and has since had a vasectomy. I can't help but feel jealous and angry that it came so easy to them. Two kids within 3 years. I can't even manage one in that time. It's put a great strain on our friendship at times. The Facebook posts of how wonderful it is to be a dad, the what feels like patronising "don't worry, you'll find out one day" speeches, the spending time with his kids meaning we miss out on watching the big match together. It just felt like a needle in the heart every time. Every time I'd see another Facebook update, I'd get angry and want to throw my iPad against the wall or chuck my phone down the toilet. It wasn't his fault, I get that, but I questioned his loyalty, his selfishness for not thinking about my feelings but at the end of the day he wasn't not doing what any other new parent does.

A lot of these feelings have since subsided but they do rear their ugly head from time to time.

My wife, my love, she has been great throughout the whole process. It's been a generally sad time, with some happy moments but she's been a strength to me, whether she knows it or not. We've probably grown a lot closer and stronger for it. It's us against the world as we say.

When we realised a baby may or may not happen, we decided to expand the family in other ways. We decided to get another dog. So, in August last year we picked up our little dude of a chihuahua. He might be a menace from time to time but we couldn't be without him and it puts a huge smile on our faces to see how much he dotes on our other dog. Early this year we also decided to move home. We had originally lived in Aberdeen before moving 40 miles north to be out of the city life, and it was also so that we could get a house with a garden and be closer to my family. Baby preparation time! That's obviously all fallen through and because of the toll the commute was taking on my wife, we made the decision to move back to town. When the move was becoming a reality, it hit home how gut-wrenching it was that our family plans hadn't come to fruition. It was a happy but sad time all in one. However, now it seems like the best decision we made because we both couldn't be happier living back in the city, closer to our friends and in a place where it's a lot easier to do things as the choices are greater. I'll forever miss that beach though.

We have now officially begun NHS- funded IVF treatment. Any day now, Mrs I will start taking the tablets in preparation for the next step. Everyone has been very supportive. Very caring and thoughtful. The clinic has been wonderful and I couldn't thank them enough. We've not been to any counselling or group sessions but that may come as the process goes on.

My closest friends have been there to lean on as has my family. Even my best mate with the kids. I've felt very awkward discussing things with them but it's got a little easier over time. We've had a lot of sympathy and empathy but sometimes it's unwanted because they've never gone through this themselves. I probably shouldn't feel like that but it can't be helped sometimes."

P - *"The guilt consumed me. For so long, I assumed it wasn't anything to do with me, because although you read about things like a low sperm count, you don't know what it means until it happens to you. The worst part was the look on my wife's face. Because we had both mentally prepared for it to just be something that was wrong with her, and now she was looking at me like she pitied me. It really hurt.*

We went through the motions that most couples did. At first, we comforted one another (her comforting me mostly, which made me feel like less of a man. One thing I know now is that tears don't mean shit to her, she loves me even if I'm a sap), and me shutting her out because I felt like I couldn't give her the one thing she wanted. The doctors said that there were things we could do. I cried a lot, but I tried not to in front of her, which lead to a lot of forced conversations to break the silence which seemed to hang over us. I even cried on the phone to my dad. He didn't really know what to do. Then we fought a lot, mainly because I was angry with myself. She said I was pushing her away, and maybe I was, but it was only because I felt like she deserved better than me. It was a really hard time between the diagnosis and the first appointment for treatment, because there isn't much information or forums online, men just don't seem to talk about it.

When we eventually went back to the doctor to start treatment, that was a bit of a turning point for us. We knew we were in this together, and that the only way we would get through it was as a team. We went through IUI (Intrauterine insemination) and fell pregnant on our first go, but sadly it wasn't meant to be. We were very fortunate to have a very strong and sympathetic fertility team who were extremely helpful. We tried again around 6 months later, and now we have a beautiful little boy. He is our world. I'm so proud of my wife for going through this with me, and not once did she ever blame me, even when I blamed myself. She had to go through some pretty uncomfortable procedures, and there were times when we were close to breaking point, but I can honestly say it made us a stronger team, and I love her even more for going through this with me".

A – America, Married. "We were really shocked when we found out we both had fertility problems. My wife has PCOS, so we knew we were up against it. However, when we were told that I had a low sperm count too, it was as though someone was saying "look, it's not meant to be". To give you our back story, we have been together for 9 years, and we have always said we wanted to have children. We got married 3 years ago, and on our wedding night we were convinced we would get pregnant straight away. We did not. Then my wife was referred to a hospital specialist and underwent a laparoscopy for PCOS. We went to the fertility specialist kind of knowing it was going to be an uphill struggle, but when the doctor turned to me and told me "Mr D, you have a very low sperm count." I kind of zoned out. We went home and my wife was very upset, and seeing her cry broke my heart.

We went through 2 years of trying for a baby via IVF, and it was hell. My wife felt so ill throughout it, and I couldn't really do much for her, apart from be there for her. We lost one baby at 17 weeks, and it was a dark time in our house. The idea of having a baby consumed my wife, and when she was having a bad day it made me feel even worse. I suffered badly with depression, and felt so trapped. I mean, it's not really something you discuss with your mates at the pub, is it? So, I became somewhat introverted and alienated from my friends...

Cutting a long story short, we are now pregnant again, but it's not been easy. We are both very excited by also nervous because we lost one of our babies before. We have just got to 14 weeks so the next few weeks are going to be testing times, but we feel like we are better prepared this time. All I can say to any guys who read this, is that your partner is the one person who is going through this with you, and I don't think men realize that if we have a low count or problems it's still going to mean she's going through something pretty shitty - you've still got to get that little balls of cells inside her, and it's not nice! You've gotta make sure you go through this together and support one another. Not once did my wife ever blame me for anything, and although we had some horrible days, having her support means everything to me, and I just want to do all I can for her and our baby. Even if it takes the rest of my life to show how much I appreciate what she has done for us".

For this book, I have had to do some research into male infertility. You know what? It was really bloody hard to find anything other than the scientific jargon and the treatments available. I know guys don't really like the whole touchy-feely stuff, but it's pretty shitty that there isn't very much information or forums on the subject. Maybe I just wasn't looking in the right places? Who knows.

Maybe it's like some sort of secret underground society whereby you need the required body parts to be allowed in. All the men I spoke to said that they felt really isolated and that they couldn't really talk to anyone about it, so, if you (or indeed your partner) are in this boat, IVF Babble and the Infertility Network both have dedicated forums and Facebook pages for men. Everyone needs some support, and on the shittiest days, you still need somewhere to vent. If you can't talk to your man friends about this, or your parents, and you feel you're driving your partner crazy talking about your swimmers (or lack of, depending on your situation), please consider maybe talking to people in these forums/groups. It's 2017 guys. It's OK to talk about your feelings, like it's OK to moisturize and cry. We are all human.

Ladies. If your man is diagnosed with infertility problems, please for the love of all things great and small, do not point the finger. Do not make them feel like this is all their fault, and do not patronize them. Because if they did it to you, you would feel like shit, and probably resent them for it. You're going to have a family together, you're a team, so act like it.

So that's the end of this short chapter. Please don't take offense that I've kept it short and sweet, because a lot of what happens on the road to a BFP (that's a Big Fat Positive) is a joint effort. The next few chapters will (hopefully) show that. But I thought it was important to address this on its own, because hey, it's takes two to tango, right?

Act Five - IUI and IVF - The long road to getting a positive

Brace yourselves guys. This is going to be one heck of a chapter. We are going into some pretty complex territory, I'll do my best to keep it as simple as I can, but it's going to be quite sciencey.

So, you've waited the obligatory 12 months. You've spent more money on ovulation kits and pregnancy tests online than you have on your mobile phone bill. (I use that example as in one month I've spent the equivalent of MY phone bill on the above. Then I discovered you can buy them on amazon for £3 for 20.) You've driven yourself and your partner bananas with tests and talking about the top ten things you can do to get pregnant. You've even started yoga and taking folic acid. There are babies everywhere you go, and when you go to lunch with your friends and one of them just passes you their gorgeous, gurgly, absolutely cutest-kid-you've-seen-in-your-life (except for every other of your friends and families' offspring, but you get the point) 18-month-old your heart just melts. The sight of seeing your beloved with said little bubba reduces you to a pile of gooey broody mush.

You've been for your initial tests with your GP, and you've been referred to a fertility specialist. After the first round of tests with them, which have come back with one result or another that concludes that yes, there is a "problem" with either yours, his, or indeed both of your reproductive tool kits. You may have already been on a cycle of Clomid in an attempt to boost your egg production. Speaking to those who have been through these procedures this seems to be the first thing people are offered. If that doesn't work, you'll have to go back and potentially have more testing done. Now that's all out of the way, you've been sat down in your consultant's office. Niceties have been exchanged, and you've been told that you have a couple of choices of treatment to get pregnant.

In the red corner, you have IUI. otherwise known as Intrauterine Insemination.

In the blue corner, you have IVF. this is known as In-vitro Fertilization.

So, what is the difference between the two?

Let's start with IUI.

Intrauterine Insemination, or IUI, is a fertility treatment that involves placing sperm inside the womb to facilitate fertilization. Sounds easy, right?

Not really. Allow me to explain, with the help of the infertility network and first-hand accounts from people I have spoken to. I've not been through this procedure myself, so please bear with me if it gets a bit scienc-ey.

IUI is still a complex procedure, where timing is the key and there are a couple of different types you can have, depending on your own situation. You have your "natural insemination", where the procedure is performed around your natural ovulation cycle. You also have "Stimulated insemination" where the procedure is planned around particular fertility treatments. These will have been used hand in hand with the procedure, such as drugs to stimulate egg production.

IUI is usually offered if your male accomplice has sluggish swimmers. The procedure involves taking his sample, "washing" (the fluid accompanying the little guys is removed, and the faster moving and better formed ones are separated from the slower ones) and then taking these and placing them directly inside your womb via a catheter type needle. Think of it like a smear test, with a little extra pain thrown in for good measure.

If you are having this procedure on a natural insemination basis, it can be quite straightforward. From the ladies' point of view, there won't be any extra medication for you to take. The procedure will be performed between days 12-16 of your cycle, depending on when your ovulation takes place. However, that by no means makes it an easy process. That's because for this to happen you need to know when you are ovulating. This means blood tests, ultrasounds, and urine tests to pinpoint when this time of the month is. If you are not ovulating frequently or regularly, this could make things a bit more difficult. Ugh.

Enter "Stimulated Insemination"! So, with this procedure from what I can gather, you will be given drugs to stimulate egg production to start with. This will be along the lines of Clomid, (I'll go into a bit more about these in a bit) which will help to stimulate your little egg making machines to produce more follicles. While you are taking this, you will have regular ultrasounds - both the traditional and trans-vaginal, or internal - to keep an eye on them. There will be blood tests to ensure you are ovulating and to track exactly when this takes place and to check the development of your eggs. Once they have matured, you will be given a hormone injection to stimulate their release. This is the trigger point for insemination, around 36-60 hours later. It's go time people! Let's make a baby!

Once you know when this is happening, your man will need to get reacquainted with that plastic beaker again. The doctors will then take his sample, which will be washed, and the rapidly moving sperm will be separated out from the slower ones. If you are using donated or frozen sperm, it will be removed from frozen storage, thawed and prepared in the same way. You will both be prepared (mentally for both, physically for you) for the procedure. This will probably be at your fertility clinic, but depending on your area you may be at your local hospital (if for example, your clinic isn't located at your hospital).

On the big day, the doctor will first insert a speculum, (sorry to be so clinical but there's no other way to describe it. Being cranked open with a car jack? No. bad imagery there. How about a joke to lighten the mood? One ovary says to the other ovary, "Hey, did you order any furniture?" The other ovary says, "No, why?" "There are a couple of nuts outside trying to shove an organ in." you're welcome.) as in a smear test to keep your, ahem, walls apart. A small catheter type needle (a sort of soft, flexible tube) will then be threaded into your womb via your cervix. The best-quality sperm will be selected and inserted through the catheter. If his very best swimmers are still a little on the slow side, they will be flushed in with some extra liquid to help ensure they flow to the eggs easier and quicker.

That got pretty technical, huh? Bear with me, because this will be quite a technical chapter. There's lots of science involved in assisted fertility. More than I realized - this has been an eye opener for me, so I'm sure it will be for you too!

The whole process only takes a few minutes and is usually painless, although some women have said they experienced a temporary, menstrual-like cramping. It's important to keep as calm and your muscles as relaxed as possible. Any tension will only make things more difficult and painful - remember, your cervix is only an inch wide, and your doctor will need to ensure the tube is inserted steadily. It's kind of like threading a needle, which carries your precious cargo. So, keep calm and the doctor can ensure the sperm is deposited in the right place. The more relaxed you are, the easier it will be. Gents, Fellas, Lads, Men, please stay by your lady's side throughout this, because you being there will probably help her be more relaxed. Besides, it's a team effort, right? (however, if she would prefer to be in there on her own don't force your presence upon her). After the procedure, you will likely have another ultrasound to ensure the little guys are where they need to be, and you will be given a debrief on what to expect over the coming days.

You may want to rest for a short time before going home, where you are going to want to rest a lot more. This is not the time for doing an extreme spin class or CrossFit, this is a time for relaxing, resting and taking it easy (this advice is more for the ladies, but guys, we know how you like to think you're helping by sympathising, so after you've made her tea, run a bath or whatever she would prefer, feel free to relax too - your work is done!). Think along the lines of good book and cake. Cake is always the correct answer (see, we are getting to know one another!). Sex should be off the cards for the next few days as it could be a bit on the painful side, but if you feel up for it, I guess that's all good. You will then have to wait two weeks before you can do a pregnancy test, either at home, or at your clinic. This is commonly known as the Two-Week Window. It'll be a long two weeks, however it will go a lot quicker if you try and distract your mind from things, as difficult as it will be.

In itself, this procedure sounds like it is normally quite straightforward. From what I've been told, it is usually fairly painless, although you may experience mild cramps similar to period pains like I mentioned. You will not require to stay in hospital, though a day or two off work is completely understandable.

However as with all clinical procedures there are risks associated with the fertility drugs that are often used with this treatment. These can include reactions to the drugs and certain pregnancy problems, such as your ovaries going into overdrive, aka Hyperstimulation. I'll go into this later. With stimulated IUI, you also run the risk of multiple pregnancy - where more than one egg is fertilised. This results in non-identical twins which in themselves come with a whole host of pregnancy related complications. The use of ultrasound scanning before ovulation means that if there are more than two mature egg follicles present, the cycle can be abandoned. This eliminates the risk.

(not that twins are a bad thing, absolutely not.)

So how successful is IUI?

Success rates depend on the cause and severity of the infertility and your age. UK success rates for IUI add up to around:
- *16 per cent if you are under 35*
- *11 per cent if you are between 35 and 39*
- *five per cent if you are between 40 and 42*
- *one per cent if you are between 43 and 44*
- *0 nought per cent if you are over 44*

Not great. 16% at the best. Sigh.

The plus side is in the UK couples are recommended up to six cycles of treatment. This is usually reserved for unexplained infertility or mild endometriosis, or if you have a low sperm count. That does not mean you will get 6 cycles. Not every postcode area offers the same cycles, some are funded, some aren't, so it's worth checking all of this with your clinic first. If you keep trying for up to six times you do increase your chances of becoming pregnant by up to 50%.

If you decide to go private, it's can be pretty costly. As a guide, these are some quoted costs:
- *IUI using Partner Sperm £700*
- *IUI using Donor Sperm £1295*
- *Induction of Ovulation (excludes drugs) with IUI with partner £1085*
- *Induction of Ovulation (excludes drugs) with IUI with donor sperm £1835*
- *Drugs Approximately per cycle of Induction of ovulation £200- £350*

Providing you hit all the criteria, you will be offered the recommended 6 cycles via the NHS depending on your local CCG criteria. It's important to bear in mind that treatments are offered on the NHS across the board, and your local areas criteria will be stricter than NICE. The availability of artificial insemination on the NHS varies throughout the UK. In some areas, the waiting list for treatment can be very, very long and in others it's not offered, hence why some people choose to go private straight away. I'll go into the postcode lottery later.

IUI can be pretty frustrating:

"I went for my 11-day scan on the Tuesday and it turned out I had 9 follicles. 9! The nurse said I had reacted too well the drugs and I was too fertile, so they wouldn't go ahead with the procedure that month. I felt so disappointed I nearly cried in front of the nurse, I'd have to start again the following month but they had to reduce the dosage of the drugs I take. It was so frustrating. We went from being infertile to too fertile and back again for months!"

"My first round of IUI was a nightmare. We went in full of positive vibes, but came away slightly disappointed. It started off well. I had 3 good sized follicles and his sample was good, but the nurse had trouble getting the catheter through my cervix. She said I have '2 doors' so to speak. I had no idea whether that is normal or common. (I did have a feeling that there would be trouble because I couldn't have to hycosy test because of the same problem, so had to have a laparoscopy.) So anyway, to reduce anymore trauma she decided to implant the sample in between the '2 doors' (those were her words). She said it's not the ideal place, but it is further than it would normally get. So, I can still be hopeful. I realize now that this was probably the reason that I did not become pregnant. I have been researching and I think I may have a posterior cervix. I had to wait the agonizing 2 weeks, but the nurse said that if it didn't work this time, then next attempt would be done in theatre where they have better equipment to be able to get around it. "

"Years ago, my first IUI was successful! It only took 1 to get my beautiful daughter. Unfortunately, ttc baby number two has been more difficult. 5 IUIs so far (4 negatives and 1 miscarriage)."

But, for some couples, it can be the answer to all their problems:

"In January, I had my first IUI (with Clomid, Gonal-F, Ovidrel) but it was my 5th medicated cycle. My first IUI was a success! My diagnosis was anovulation. I think statistically, you have the best chance of success with IUI the first 3 times."

"It can happen! We were extremely lucky that the first IUI worked for us. I only had one mature follicle and it worked! I have PCOS, my husband has no problems. To all my infertile ladies, stay hopeful."

"We had been TTC for two and a half years both naturally and with clomid. All of our tests were fine. We had tried clomid alone for many cycles with nothing. Our first IUI with clomid landed us with twins! It can happen."

So, there we have it. We are IUI Jedi's now.

So, what about IVF?

"After realizing that the only way we'd have any chance of attempting a pregnancy was going to be via IVF, the world became a pretty difficult place for a while. At this point we knew any NHS funding would not be available to us due to the criteria set in our area. We could tick every box, except the one which asks, "do you or your partner have any children?"
My husband's two boys. Despite not living with us this meant that we - with the fertility issue being mine - would not receive any financial help towards treatment."

This is going to be a particularly emotional section, because the stories I have received regarding IVF pulled at my heartstrings. I have not been through this, but I may well have to, so think of this as a learning curve for both you, the reader, and I the writer. We are in this one together. There will be some excerpts from a couple of ladies, and I'm sorry in advance if there is more on IVF than IUI, but it appears that IVF is what you get if:

- *You both have fertility issues*
- *You Have PCOS, Endometriosis or PID*
- *You have tried follicle inducing medication, and IUI with no success*

The good news is that you can get IVF on the NHS, but you have to meet NHS criteria which is set by NICE, is as follows:

" 1.11.1.3 In women aged under 40 years who have not conceived after 2 years of regular unprotected intercourse or 12 cycles of artificial insemination (where 6 or more are by intrauterine insemination), offer 3 full cycles of IVF, with or without ICSI. If the woman reaches the age of 40 during treatment, complete the current full cycle but do not offer further full cycles."

However, the final decision about who can have NHS-funded IVF in England is made by local Clinical Commissioning Groups (CCGs). Their criteria are going to stricter than those recommended by NICE. It's worth checking with your doctor to see what the criteria is in your area. For example, in our post code area, couples are only offered two funded cycles of IVF. That made me cry quite a lot, because for years I've clung to the idea of having three chances, but no one has ever told me different until I went to a group counselling session. Other postcode areas, such as in Essex, don't offer any funding. Some places such as in Scotland offer up to three cycles. It's all dependent on the funding available in your area which if you ask me is unethical and cruel and just unnecessary. So again, please check your local CCG criteria.

If you can't afford to go private and decide to go via NHS at a specific clinic, you will have to hit the CCGs criteria. We went to a support group evening at Southampton's Complete Fertility Clinic, (It is free and open to anyone to go to, which is awesome.) which does accept NHS patients who meet their rather strict criteria. To be considered, you must:

- Comply with NICE Clinical Practice and have gone through the primary and secondary care subfertility pathways appropriate to them before IVF is considered. I clicked on the link and presented with some of the most complex flow diagrams with the longest winded technical descriptions I've ever seen. And I can do technical. I work in IT projects. Note to doctors - MAKE IT EASY TO UNDERSTAND PLEASE. We are confused as it is.

- The following investigations must all have been completed prior to referral:
- Rubella,
- Chlamydia,
- Hepatitis B, Hepatitis C and HIV.

- *Have had infertility of at least 1 to 2 years duration*
  Couples with a diagnosed cause of "absolute infertility" which eliminates any possibility of getting pregnant naturally, and who meet all the other criteria, will have a fast pass to IVF. All other couples must have infertility of at least 1 to 2 years duration. 2 years!

- *The woman must be 34 years or below at time of referral;*
  The age at referral should be before the female's 35th birthday. Women approaching the age of 35 years must be referred in time to be able to commence treatment before their 35th birthday. After this, you will have to pay.

- *Never have received NHS funded IVF/ICSI treatment or have had more than 2 self-funded cycles of IVF/ICSI and have no frozen embryos stored from a previous cycle.*

- *Women in same sex couples or women not in a partnership must be sub-fertile*
  (10 unsuccessful cycles of IUI as evidence of unexplained infertility).

- *Not have a living child (including adopted) from their relationship, or any previous relationship. - I don't get why this is a problem. Having a child from another relationship does not automatically make them your child, and you won't be their parent.*

- *Not have been sterilized for either partner.*

- *Have a BMI range between 19 and 29.9 for at least the last six months.*

- *Both be non-smokers for at least the last six months.*
So just a small list, right?

As long as you tick all the boxes, you will be eligible for NHS funded IVF, up to three cycles (again this is dependent on your area). If you decide to go private you will still have to comply with a number of these factors, namely to do with health and lifestyle.

If you are in very very good circumstances, you can of course go private, but then you can be looking at costs up to £6,000 plus for private IVF. Sounds crazy, right? Here's a breakdown, per cycle, of some of the costs quoted for IVF:

Consultations:
- Initial consultation £185
- Review consultation £115
- Counselling service for first 2 sessions No charge
- Additional counselling sessions £50

In Vitro Fertilisation (IVF) Treatment
- IVF £3190
- Time-Lapse Embryoscope in addition to IVF £680
- Intracytoplasmic Sperm injection (ICSI) in addition to IVF £1100
- Approximate price of drugs per cycle for IVF £750-£1600

HFEA Licence Fee
- HFEA fee for IVF/Frozen Embryo Transfer/Egg Recipient/Egg Sharing £80
- HFEA fee for using donor sperm £37.50

Frozen Embryo Transfer
- Transfer of frozen embryos £1120
- Transfer of donated frozen embryo cycle £3245
- Drugs for hormone controlled Frozen Embryo Transfer £200-£300

Freezing and Storage
- Egg Freezing (excludes drugs) £3360
- Semen Freezing £300
- Subsequent semen samples £200

- *Embryo freezing (Includes free storage for 1 year) £350*
- *Subsequent storage (up to 2 years) £250*

Pretty crazy huh? If someone can explain to me why having a child in a previous relationship means you should have to fork out all this, I'd be happy to listen. It scares me that you only get three cycles on the NHS if you are lucky and live in an area that offers it. Thanks to 90% of Clinical Commissioning Groups across the country, most regions only offer 1 cycle. one. that's it. What then?

Not everyone can afford that sort of money. Some people will decide to go abroad to try and save money, one couple I spoke with has considered Greece, Cyprus, Spain, because it's so much cheaper. Several clinics overseas offer a money back guarantee, whereby you pay for 3-4 cycles up front and if you don't fall pregnant because of these, you will get your money back.

My only advice on this is to make sure you do your research thoroughly on the clinic. Make sure they are part of the EU medical association, consider the success rates. Try and go to visit them beforehand, make sure there are English speaking doctors and nurses available. Find out what procedures are offered; do they offer donor eggs (which is a much easier option if you are going overseas). There's a lot to take in and It's a huge gamble but for some it's a more affordable option. The other option is moving to an area in the UK that offers the recommended three cycles.

So, what exactly happens when you go through the IVF shenanigans?

Well, it's pretty long process.
Firstly, you have to go through the many many rounds of blood testing, ultrasounds and other such tests to make sure you're actually ovulating. This can also mean you will need to take/administer a number of drugs to help this process along. You need to keep having ultrasounds - both the traditional cold jelly on the belly and a roller ball type contraption over your stomach, and the internal (or wonderfully named trans vaginal) type, where a sort of probe is inserted - to make sure your uterus wall lining is thick enough to ensure you can take this medication too.

The whole process can take a while. From what I have been told around 5mm is the optimum thickness to be aiming for. If it's too thick, or too thin, you can't continue with the process, which can take MONTHS.

Once you have reached the goldilocks of wall lining - not too thick, not too thin, but just right - you can start taking the medication to help you to produce some beautiful follicles. Follicles are the little sacs your eggs will develop in- yippee! But at any stage, that pesky lining can mess it all up and you'll have to wait ANOTHER month before you can move to the next step. If anything, IVF helps develop your patience levels.

Once you have the right level, and you've managed to keep it that way, you can take the medication. Once you have started the medication, you'll also get used to needles, because you have to administer the injections every day. And you'll need scans every week or so to make sure everything is behaving. One of the worst things that can happen is your ovaries can go into overdrive, or hyperstimulation, most commonly abbreviated to OHSS (Ovarian Hyper Stimulation Syndrome) which is a bad reaction to the medication. Overstimulated ovaries enlarge and release chemicals into the bloodstream that make blood vessels leak fluid into the body. Fluid leaks into your abdomen and, in severe cases, into the space around the heart and lungs. OHSS can affect the kidneys, liver and lungs. A serious, but rare, complication is a blood clot (thrombosis). A very small number of deaths have been reported. As many as 1 in three women will develop OHSS. In most cases your ovaries will resolve themselves within a few days of rest, drinking plenty of fluids and mild pain relief.
More severe cases may require hospital treatment. You can still continue with the egg retrieval if your case is not deemed so serious that you have to go to hospital. One lady told me she had over 50 follicles, which were retrieved. They just can't put them back in until your ovaries have calmed down.

So, you're well on your way to making some beautiful little follicles, now what?

Egg Retrieval!

This is when the doctors will physically remove the eggs. You will normally be sedated, so you shouldn't feel much, but you will be awake for the procedure. In some cases, you will be put under general anaesthetic, if that's the case, don't panic, because it's not unusual.

On the day, your partner will need to deposit a donation (aka semen collection) too, so it'll be a pretty big day for the two of you. During your procedures, it might help you feel more comfortable having one another in the room with you, and most clinics will encourage it. Remember, this is a team effort, so support one another throughout! The procedure itself is pretty straight forward - a needle is passed through the top of the vagina under ultrasound guidance to get to the ovary and follicles.

The fluid in the follicles is aspirated through the needle and the eggs detach from the follicle wall and are sucked out of the ovary. It's usually completed in around half an hour, depending on how many follicles you have to remove. Afterwards, you'll probably take a while to come around completely and I would say you definitely will have earned a couple of days off. Go team!

So, once you go home, your lovely eggs and his handsome little swimmers will be whisked off to a lab to be formally introduced. With a little helping hand of the lab technicians of course. (a shout out to all the lab techs who work in chilled laboratories mixing babies - you rule).

The fluid with the eggs is passed to the IVF lab where the eggs are identified, rinsed, and placed in small drops in plastic culture dishes. The dishes with the eggs are then kept in specialized IVF incubators under carefully controlled environmental conditions.

The sperm will be washed to remove the seminal fluid, and the best in show will be used to fertilize your eggs. Now this is a bit of a numbers game, (baby making is a numbers game) because say you produce 25 follicles. Out of those 25, only 15 might be healthy enough to fertilize. Of those 15, only 9 might successfully fertilize, and of those 9 only 4 might survive the whole process and form what they call a blastocyst stage.

This can take 3-5 days. Once those little guys are ready, you'll have them put back in again. These number drops are very common and completely natural. Not all eggs are created equally, some are stronger than others. The cells don't divide properly, there could be chromosome problems, or they can just behave erratically. It's natural selection at its finest.

Sometimes none of the eggs will fertilize, and I'm sorry to say that means you will need to start the whole process again. (insert sad face here). But, providing they do survive, you get to advance to the next level.

So around 5 days after egg retrieval, your little blastocysts will be put back into your womb to burrow down and start developing. (This is sometimes done on day three depending on the strength of the blastocyst and weather the lab technicians think it will survive another 2 days in the culture dish. If you have a day three egg put back in, this is not abnormal) This is done in a similar way to the retrieval, with a catheter type needle and ultrasound and your partner by your side. Because it's a little less stressful on your body and the needle doesn't go as far into your insides, you might not be put under anaesthetic, but you will be given some form of pain relief. I'm going to insert a funny here, because this comment really made me giggle when I read it:

"So many of these processes need to be done with a full bladder; keeping your bladder full and not entirely losing the remaining scraps of your dignity by peeing on anyone should be an Olympic sport and I'd be a contender to represent my country."

So once the little guys are back inside, safely deposited in your lovely womb lining, you get to go through the longest wait of your life. Most couples going through fertility treatment fear the time frame described in these next three words.

Two. week. Wait.

This is the two-week window where you are in PUPO, or pregnant until proven otherwise. You have to wait until the two weeks are up before any blood tests or pregnancy tests can be done to provide an accurate result. Lots of people I have spoken to told me how hard these two weeks were and how they tried to fill those two weeks with as many activities as possible to pass the time.

Imagine it's like you've been for a job interview. You had a great telephone interview, you aced the first and second face to face interview. You've been out for a meet the team drinks to get to know the people you may or may not be working with, and as you're walking out the door, you are told "oh by the way, we won't be in touch for two weeks with our decision". It's enough to drive even the most patient person insane. But my advice and the advice from the many people I have spoken to is to go on with your life as normal. Go to work, go for walks, read, go out for tea and cake (eat a fuck load of cake, eat the whole damn thing if you want.) take long baths, go swimming (maybe stay away from overly strenuous exercise, now is not the time to start training for a marathon), visit family, enjoy your time together. Don't put your life on hold for two weeks - it'll go much faster if you just let the time flow, even though it will feel like time is standing still.

After the two weeks are up, things can go one of two ways, but they both start the same. You'll need to go back to the clinic for a blood test, and then wait for the results. This is normally on the same day, and again, it's going to feel like time is standing still for that day - go to see a movie, eat more cake (you can never ever have too much, and if anyone says any different, fuck them they don't know your shit and have no right to invade on you and your cake time). After those 21,600 seconds (or 6 hours to me and you), you'll get a call and it will be one of the following:

A negative result means it has not been successful. This means that for whatever reason, the egg did not develop. Now I cannot stress enough to you, and even though you'll probably tell me to piss off, please please please do not blame yourself. These things happen, and we cannot guarantee that everything will always work the way you want it to. You will probably be asked to go back to your clinic to discuss the next steps, which may mean you will need to start again. This might mean just from egg implanting, if you had eggs frozen, or egg retrieval, which means starting the whole process again. I think it's important to stress here that it's nothing you can change. It's nothing to do with what you did or didn't do, it's all down to the embryo and whether it was 100%. You can't blame yourself for something outside of your control.

A positive result, means you are freaking pregnant. With child. A bun in the oven. Preggo. This is celebration time - woot woot! You will need to go back to your clinic to go through your next steps and unless you decide to stay private, you'll probably go on to be a bog-standard NHS maternity patient, although I'm sure if you wanted to speak to someone at your clinic they would be happy to do so.

The whole process of IVF sounds terrifying, confusing, exhausting and just mind boggling. It can be the biggest roller coaster you go through as a couple. The tears, the injections, the exhaustion, everything can be a bit overwhelming at times, and for some, it just doesn't work the way it's supposed to. A lot of the women I spoke to have been through the process a few times before they got the positive call, and it is tiring!

What I have learned the most from listening to other people's stories, and what I found really comforting is how the whole experience brought them together closer as a couple. There's no stereotypical role playing, in that us ladies cry our eyes out and the gents in our lives try and fix it, because you both have a massive role to play in this process.

And really there's nothing to be fixed. You're not broken. You aren't dying. Your life isn't going to end because you can't have children. It's just that the emotional distress of imagining your life without children is too much to bear to the point that it can break even the strongest women (and men) that you can't bear the pain, and you have to do something about it. That's what infertility is at the heart. It's not a death sentence. It feels like a life sentence. And you are given the options to help this work, and to get through this. Sometimes it works, sometimes it doesn't.

But you are still here. And if it doesn't work, and you can't have children, or you have a successful IVF cycle and then the next time you try it doesn't happen, you can't just stop living your own life. You must try to move past the raw emotional pain and make peace with yourself. Because otherwise you will put your life on hold and lose yourself.

Why is there such a stigma?

Over the last couple of years, I have come to terms with my infertility problems. I am not ashamed of it, it's part of who I am. I know it's going to be tough, and I (think) I'm mentally prepared for the uphill struggle. But why is there such a stigma around being infertile, and in turn, having to go through IVF?

The main reason I decided to write this book, is because it feels a little bit like you are in some underground secret society when you are infertile. It's a bit like, you can't just talk about it to your friends. Because they sometimes look at you like you have some sort of terminal illness that they can't do anything about (like I said before, it's not a disease) and it can be hard for people to get their heads around. But why is there such a stigma? And what can you do? Where do you go? Online?

Well, I'd be lying if I said there wasn't any support or help available online. In fact, there are a load of websites, forums and help pages for people going through this process, but they can be daunting places. There is something both glutinous and ghoulish about these forums.

It's a euphemistic world where the language of relationships is made to feel infantile and many a creepy acronym is adopted. There are no boyfriends or husbands, only 'DH' (dear husband) for even the most useless of men. Rather than being wished luck, you are 'sent baby dust' and women's tales of miscarriage are peppered with tragicomic flying-baby emoticons. You can find yourself spending hours trying to navigate your way through the BFNs and the BFPs (that's big fat negative and big fat positive) and my personal favourite (it's not, it's horrid) BD (baby dance — yes, that's sex) to try to make sense of your experience.

The forums make me wish all the more that we could as a society and as human beings, talk more openly and sensibly about infertility. These women online are clearly tough cookies, there is no doubt about that; they've endured numerous, arduous treatment cycles, not to mention miscarriages. Yet online they communicate in somewhat infant and babyish voices. We do everyone a disservice by being coy. We are fucking superhuman, so why can't we act like it and stop putting so much pressure on ourselves to be "perfect". Infertility is all consuming for some women, me included. Mrs S below describes the feelings perfectly:

"When I had unknown fertility problems before being referred it was awful... This is how I felt:
Despite 6.5 years of hard graft, work & emotions, the gut wrenching feeling of "I don't think I'm ever going to get pregnant but I can't believe it" is all too much. This is the first time I've failed and it's totally beyond my control to do anything about it. What have I done wrong? I don't know how to face anyone else knowing this and I don't know how to face myself. I think I might break.

That sounds dramatic but remember this is cumulative - this is 6.5 years of failing every month - that's 78 months of failing, plus hearing baby announcements, plus questions, plus 546 times of worrying/ doubting / thinking every single day. Plus, life happening all around - snapping my Achilles, stress & off work, redundancy twice. Worrying about my relationship, constantly worrying about sex. And no one talks about it, fertility problems are hidden, secret, unspeakable. No one wants to talk of failure, no one wants to hear about failure.

It was the worst thing I'd ever been through and at one point I became really unstable in my thinking (I never voiced them out loud) - I didn't want to see friends, I was jealous of people with children & pregnancies. I Thought some truly awful things. I hated my friends and family for not understanding, although I could never be open with them about what was happening to me so how could they be?"

If we talked about it more, we'd all know that fertility treatment is available on the NHS and rightly so. It's not something that is exclusively available to the wealthy, nor is it a privilege. It's a rollercoaster or emotional distress that not every woman can go through. With fewer people able to buy a home in their twenties, more women working and life expectancy increasing, it's only going to get more common for women to have children later in life.

And what about all the advice online. What and who can you trust. In researching for this book, I have come across some weird, wonderful and downright worrying websites offering this so-called help and advice, and it's not free half the time. There are websites offering a miracle all in one multi vitamin to help increase sperm production. Others which sell CDs full of soothing music to help you to relax your womb to prepare it for motherhood. Smoothies, shakes, pills, creams, everything you can think of. Which sex positions. Which food to eat. Which foods not to eat. The best time of day, how long to do it for.

NONE OF IT MATTERS.

It's utter bollocks. Sorry, but it is. You can't fall for all this schmuck if you want to keep your sanity intact. If you want facts, go to HEFA, The British Fertility Society, The Fertility Network, The NHS. Ask your fertility specialist. Us fertility challenged bunch are an extremely vulnerable lot, and unfortunately, there are people out there who will want to monetize our misfortune. Don't believe all you read online, talk to a professional.

By the way, bananas don't improve sperm count, and having sex upside down against a wall at the dawn of the 3rd Sunday doesn't improve your chances, no matter how soothing the womb music is.

So, what can you do?

GO TO A COUNSELLING SESSION.

Do you know how good it feels to sit in a room of people who are all in the same boat as you, both men and women, and be able to tell one another how much you hate seeing pictures of all your friend's babies, and the guilt you feel at not being able to have a baby with your dearly beloved, that you feel jealous of all the baby bumps?

It feels bloody good. That what. It makes you realize that you are not going insane. That you are not being dramatic, and that you are not alone in how you feel. I think the guys found it really useful because it was one of the only places they could openly talk about the men's side of things - such as having slow swimmers, what does the inside of the "men's room" look like, how it makes them feel going through all of this, and getting a bit more of a grasp on things. For the ladies, I think it was just a comfort to know you're not being a drama queen, and this is a real thing that happens.

"I had visions of it being similar the groups frequented by Meatloaf's character in Fight Club. Someone would tell their story, then lock me in a sweaty, sobbing embrace. It wasn't like that. Alright, we were sat in a circle, but in a cosy reception area of the clinic on a Monday evening. We had a chance to introduce ourselves, and let others know our story briefly. We could ask questions of people far further along the journey than ourselves, and nod knowingly at the hurts we all experienced.

It was refreshing to be amongst other couples (not just women) who got it. Who didn't think we were selfish cows for not wanting to go to baby showers. Who hadn't seen their childhood best friends in 16 months because they'd had a baby and we just couldn't bear it. Who'd quietly unfollowed almost everyone on Facebook because we didn't want to see the "she's learned to potty train/tie her shoelaces/professionally dance ballet #blessed #proudmummy" statuses.

Those monthly meetings were something I looked forward to. We made friends, albeit ones we only saw at the meetings, we saw people leave because they'd finally fallen pregnant, we had something to get us from one childless month to the next."

I found going to these groups massively helpful, and I'm sure anyone who goes or has been would tell you what a great place they are. It helps to keep you sane, and will help get you through this long laborious process. Our little group even had a group email chain between our meetings.

The long and short of it is, if we all spoke about this more, there might not be such a huge stigma around it. Stigmas suck, and the best way to break down the barriers is to talk about it. Group sessions are a great start.

And now, for a happy ending. Remember L? Her story of her "yes" made me cry. She went through so much to get to this point. Having already been through OHSS and getting a negative after a two week wait, it proves that just because it doesn't work the first time, doesn't mean it's game over. If you are going through this process and feel like it's never ending, I hope this will help:

"At the end of February, I was going through the process of scanning my lining and tablets to prepare my body for receiving our last precious frozen embryo. I was so scared it wouldn't survive the thawing process. We had no backup, and if it didn't work, we'd have to go through the entire stimulating and collecting process we'd had in September again.

Again, on the morning of the blood test, we merrily skipped off to the clinic. I didn't know what to expect, and I nervously joked with the lovely nurse about banal things, whilst trying to prepare myself for what had to be the inevitable.
Expecting another 6 hour wait before The Phone Call, we busied ourselves by popping into a market town for a bit of rambling and distraction. My husband wandered off to find a public toilet, and I wandered around Lakeland, picking up kitchen gadgets I never knew I needed but undoubtedly had to own.

My phone rang with a Southampton area code. I went through the security questions and managed to nervously remember my date of birth and address.

Then the words came from the nurse "L, I'm pleased to say it's a positive". I can barely write that now without wanting to burst into the same tears of joy I did in Lakeland, stood by the Dyson display clutching moth sachets and a hob scraper.
I had to ask her to repeat it several times, and I have no idea how the rest of the call went.
I cried in disbelief, stood in the middle of Lakeland by myself, until a sales assistant started following me around. Clearly, I was acting suspiciously.

I went and paid for my items (I'll keep that receipt forever) and met my husband just out into the street, before I blurted out that I'd had the call and it was positive. He asked if I was joking.
Going around to tell my mum face to face was priceless. Calling my husband's parents was magical. It was his Dad's birthday, and to be able to give him that news on his 77th birthday, and to hear him properly blub down the phone was something my husband will never forget.

With an assisted pregnancy, you feel so intensely lucky and grateful, and terrified. I couldn't settle into it and enjoy it. I still can't. Those first few weeks before the early 8-week scan at the clinic were terrifying. I assumed something would go wrong. It didn't. After they were as happy as they could be, I became a standard NHS maternity patient. At each scan, and each midwife's appointment, I've felt full of trepidation, constantly wondering when my number will be up."

L is now a mum to a gorgeous little boy. He is incredible, just like his mama and papa.

Act 6 - IVF on the NHS - What it's really like on the postcode lottery.

I remember it so vividly.

Sitting at my fertility fight club in Southampton, holding cups of tea, eating cookies supplied by our (frankly, rather amazing) councillor, going around the room and talking about where we are on our journey. We try to do these things all the time, trust me. Therefore, therapy sessions are great, you get a chance to really let it all hang loose, cry ugly tears, and laugh about things other people might find awkward.

But nothing could prepare me for the huge bomb that was going to get dropped that evening.

One of the couples was talking about how they were dealing with their first two rounds failing on the NHS. They were discussing their options for their third, but they were having troubles deciding when it was going to happen because they couldn't afford it. IVF is expensive, couples can spend up to £8,000 per cycle, with only a 33% chance of success.

"But hang on, don't you get three rounds of IVF on the NHS?" I asked.

"Not in our postcode area. We only get two cycles so now we have to decide how we are going to afford our next treatment".

Note the phrase Not in Our Postcode Area. Believe it or not, it's actually really hard to get funding for IVF treatment in the UK, depending on your postcode.

Fertility Fairness is the UK's leading campaign body for this problem. For over 20 years, the charity has campaigned for people to have comprehensive and equal access to a full range of NHS funded treatments for infertility, including the right to access up to three full cycles of IVF treatment. So how is the funding decided at the moment? Can you get three cycles anywhere without re-mortgaging your home? What is the government doing about it? And what hoops do couples have to jump through to get funding?

To access funding on the NHS, depending on where you live, there are certain criteria you have to hit. Some are common sense, others are quite frankly ridiculous. As an example, I have listed below the criteria in my area (North East Hampshire) which is one of the ok-ish areas. We can get free funding for two cycles, which is defined under our CCG as "One fresh cycle and all viable frozen transfers".

I must be under 35 years old when we start treatment

Non-smokers

A BMI of 19-29.9 for a period of 6 months before receiving any sort of treatment

Been trying to conceive for 2 years

Have no previous children, dead or alive, from a previous relationship on either side.

We moved to this area with the fact that we are offered more cycles here than in Portsmouth, where it is one cycle. This information isn't even offered on the CCG websites in most cases, it's thanks to fertility fairness that I was able to find this out.

One of the downsides of IVF and needing treatment through the NHS is the plain and simple fact that for a lot of areas, the funding just isn't there anymore. It's pretty appalling really. We as a country pioneered the progress of IVF, we were the first ones to successfully give birth to a "test tube baby", yet the standards of care and the treatments available vary so much around the country. If you live in Scotland, for example, you will get three rounds of IVF funded by the NHS Scotland. If you live where I live, in Hampshire, you only get one round. If you live in Essex, then there are no rounds funded by the NHS. It's poor.

This year, the Fertility Network released the following data, amongst which key findings from The Impact of Fertility Problems 2016 with Middlesex University London stated:

90 per cent of respondents reported feeling depressed; 42% suicidal (in 1997 the figure was 20%)

54% had to pay for some or all of their treatment; 10% spending more than £30,000, some up to £100,000 (the average was £11,378; in 1997 the average was £3,466)

74% said their GP did not provide sufficient information

70% reported some detrimental effect on their relationship with their partner

75% noted the lack of a supportive workplace policy

75% would have liked to have counselling if it was free; only 44% did receive counselling and, of these, over half had to fund some of it themselves.

(There were a total of 865 responses (from predominantly women). The average age of respondents when starting fertility treatment was 32.5. Typically, respondents had been trying to conceive prior to this for 4.4 years.)

It's just not good enough. As Minister for Public Health Nicola Blackwood has stated, it is unacceptable that medical help is being denied to patients in some parts of the country. Not being able to have children is a painful and exhausting experience in itself without then being denied medical assistance, and why should having access to this treatment be exclusively reserved to those with a big enough pay packet, or those who live in the right part of the country?

Greater Manchester is the best place to live in England if you need access to free IVF, according to the national audit from campaign group Fertility Fairness. Only four out of 209 clinical commissioning group in the country follow national guidance on access to NHS fertility treatment fully and offer access to three funded cycles of IVF for eligible women under 40, plus all viable frozen embryo transfers, and enable access if one partner has a child from a previous relationship. That's less than 2 percent. All these CCGs are in the Greater Manchester area.

On the other end of the scale, Essex comes up as the worst place to live with three of the four worst CCGs, all of which have cut all NHS fertility treatments altogether; South Norfolk has also decommissioned its NHS fertility services. This apparent north-south divide extends even further: just 35 CCGs offer three NHS-funded IVF cycles in line with national guidance from NICE; 28 of these just so happen to be in northern England.

The Audit of England's 209 CCGs shows a notable reduction in access to NHS-funded IVF, with potential further cuts ahead. The number of CCGs offering three NHS-funded IVF cycles has dropped to 16 per cent, down from 24 per cent in 2013, while the number of CCGs offering one NHS-funded IVF cycle has leapt to 60 per cent up from 49 per cent in 2013. It gets worse, with more than one in ten CCGs are currently consulting on reducing or decommissioning NHS fertility treatment.

Susan Seenan, co-chair of Fertility Fairness said: *'Health minister Jeremy Hunt has said that the government will step in when people do not receive nationally-agreed standards of care. Just four out of England's 209 CCGs follow national guidance on access to NHS fertility treatment fully; the remaining 98 per cent of CCGs do not: this is cruel and unethical, and a national disgrace for the country that pioneered IVF. Infertility is a disease and women and men who cannot become parents without medical help are as deserving of healthcare as people with other medical conditions.'*

As well as slashing the number of cycles they offer, many of the CCGs are playing fast and loose with both the definition of an IVF cycle and the gruelling access criteria to IVF, and many CCGs are also creating additional eligibility criteria to further ration treatment unfairly. Almost half use their own definition of what an IVF cycle is, which typically means substantially reduced treatment is offered. These alterations hide the degree to which many CCGs are departing from national guidance.

Only ten per cent of CCGs grant funding to couples with children from a previous relationship; nine per cent deny treatment to women over the age of 35; 16 per cent stipulate couples should have been trying to conceive for three years before treatment can be offered. If a woman suffers a miscarriage during this period, the 'waiting time' clock is pretty much restarted. Other eligibility criteria include smoking status, body mass index, and length of relationship.

Put it this way:

You meet your partner when you are 25.

You get married by 29.

You start trying to have kids between 29 and 30, and then after a year realize nothing is happening. You go to your doctor who tells you that you should wait another 2 years before you are referred.

That takes you to 32-33 years of age before you get referred. That basically gives you 24 months to start a family with funding from the NHS. But what if you don't meet your partner until your 30's? Do you then rush to have kids? It's such a complex process to go through, without having to have a deadline, a BMI index, the length of time you and your partner have been together, plus a whole host of other tick box criteria put in as well!

Putting it another way, If you or your partner had an illness, and you discovered that your local NHS trust had scrapped the funding required to ensure you could get care and the only way you would receive treatment is by paying up to £12,000, or moving to an area that does offer the care on the NHS what would you do? What if you were then told you only had a 33% success rate, even if you did pay for it? This is a real problem for couples who struggle to conceive.
Being infertile is not life threatening, but the all-consuming desire to be parents, the testing, the not knowing, the constant pressure, the endless appointments, and knowing all that time it might not work is certainly life debilitating. It can destroy you as a person to fail at something every

month that others do so easily, anyone who has been through it, they will tell you how much it takes over your life. I don't know what the future holds for our attempts to have a family, but what I do know is that we only have one cycle in our area. 33%.

If you have a spare moment, please go to the fertility fairness website and email your local MP asking them to sign the petition for all CCGs to offer the three cycles of IVF recommended. Having a family shouldn't be determined to where you live or by your pay check.

Disappointingly some areas of the UK couples receive ZERO funding. In others, you receive what is classed as the "Golden Standard". If you live in Scotland, you will be offered the Gold Standard treatment. In fact, Scotland is the best place in the UK in terms of IVF provision. While Scotland will provide three funded IVF cycles for all eligible couples, and since 2010, Wales has offered women under 40 two rounds of IVF/ICSI treatment, in England both access criteria and provision of treatment are determined by postcode, and increasing numbers of Clinical Commissioning Groups are either reducing services or stopping them completely. it's an absolute minefield and even more stress to add to what is already a complex condition that affects 1 in every 3 couples in the UK. Surely, we as the pioneers of IVF should be offering patients access to a level playing field of care across the county? If someone had a heart condition would you really ration the treatment for this based on where they live?

The whole reason you should be offered three cycles is because not everyone will yield the same amount of eggs. Not all eggs are created equal. So, this puts couples in some areas at a disadvantage if their eggs aren't good enough quality to be transferred. It's emotional enough as it is without being told "This is your only chance at this, unless you have upwards of "£16-18,000 spare for other treatments". A study conducted in 2009 found that the cumulative effect of providing three full cycles of IVF increased the chances of a successful pregnancy to 45-53%. Given the upward trend in success rates, this percentage is likely to only increase over time. So why do we ration it so unfairly?

I have written to several members of parliament about this, and have received a varying degree of responses. Our old MP in Fareham Suella Fernandez simply dismissed the fact that it is unethical to ask couples to jump through these hoops, and my current MP Damien Hinds referred me to NICE guidelines and advised the following:

"I would like to reassure you that the government is following the National Institute for Health and Care Excellence (NICE) guidelines on access to IVF treatment on the NHS in England and Wales. *(It isn't)*. According to the guidelines, women aged under 40 should be offered three cycles of IVF treatment on the NHS if they have been trying to get pregnant for two years or have not been able to get pregnant after 12 cycles of artificial insemination. *(of the 20 couples, I spoke to none were offered 12 cycles of ISCI, and some CCGs restrict the age to 35, won't offer it until you have been trying for 3 years, etc.)* Provision of fertility treatment will continue to be decided at a local level by Clinical Commissioning Groups. There will be no blanket restrictions on treatment *(except for in the areas where IVF funding has been withdrawn completely)* with each case decided on an individual basis although I do understand that IVF provision can change depending on the local needs and priorities of the population. *(The priorities of the population are not a deciding factor in a couple being offered IVF)*."

I was so angered by this response. If the people who are our voices do not understand the unethical and cruel goalposts put in front of couples who just want the right to try and have children, then what chance do we have? The right to try to have a family should not be defined by your bank balance or your address. It should be fair and equal and available to all those who need it.

People often talk about their friend or friend of a friend who went through IVF and it succeeded, but people don't want to talk about how heart-breaking it is to be told "I'm sorry, we can't help you, you can't have funding". These thoughts keep me awake at night. The idea of going through IVF to be told it's not worked and there is nothing else they can do terrifies me. Because we can't afford IVF. Not many people can. But people don't recognise how debilitating it can be, because really there's nothing to be fixed. You're not broken. You aren't dying. Your life isn't going to end because you can't have children. It's just that the emotional distress of imagining your life without children is too much to bear, to the point that it can break even the strongest women (and men) and you can't bear the pain, and you must do something about it. That's what infertility is at the heart. It's not a death sentence. It feels like a life sentence. And you are given the options to help this work, and to get through this. Sometimes it works, sometimes it doesn't. But you are still here. And if it doesn't work, and you can't have children, or you have a successful IVF cycle and then the next time you try it doesn't happen, you can't just stop living your own life. You have to try to move past the raw emotional pain and make peace with yourself, and love yourself, because otherwise you will put your life on hold and lose yourself. But we need to talk about how much pressure is put on us to even get our treatment in the first place.

The postcode lottery of IVF is cruel, unethical and an added stress to many couples who so desperately wish to have a child. The only way we can get these people to understand this is to shout about it from the rooftops. You can email your MP - you might well have a much better answer than I have had from mine. You can sign the petition to get this debated in parliament again - last year 5 MP's attended a debate on the provision of IVF. 5. It's not good enough at all. You can contact your CCG (if you live in England) and copy Nicola Blackwood, Parliamentary Under Secretary of State for Public Health, in on your letters to your CCG. Contact your local Health watchdog, contact your local health and wellbeing board. And it can work. We do have a voice. There are some CCGs that have held consultations to cut funding and because of the public, it has been saved. So, we can do something about it.

To restore your faith (and ensure you keep reading) here are some great statistics for IVF success:
(Source - HEFA)

Since the first IVF baby was born in 1978, an estimated 5 million babies have been born
worldwide after IVF treatment. In the UK 240,724 babies have been born after IVF treatment
between 1991 and 2013.

The number of IVF cycles performed each year has increased steadily since 1991. The age of women seeking fertility treatment has increased since 1991, reflecting the wider trend in society for couples to start their families later, but remained steady over the last nine years.

The live birth rate after IVF has increased from only 14% in 1991, to just over a quarter by 2013.

In 2013, just over 2% of all the babies born in the UK had been conceived through IVF treatment.

One in ten babies in the UK are conceived through IVF.

Over 40% of cycles are paid for by the NHS.

Act Seven – Miscarriage

I had been putting off writing this next chapter for about 3 weeks. Mainly because we have been majorly busy, and it's a really, hard subject for me to write about. It's going to get personal here. Miscarriage is the taboo subject when it comes to pregnancy and even more so when it comes to going through assisted fertility. But for every woman, every couple who experiences this, you are so brave, so courageous, and so unbelievably awesome.

So, let's jump into it, shall we?

I've had 2 miscarriages. They were both pretty early (before 6 weeks both times), and for some I guess they don't count, because at that stage, you're not "really pregnant". It's not even formed into more than a ball of cells. But it's still heart-breaking to go through.

Both times were very similar for me, my period was late by around 10 days before I started freaking out the first time. I didn't tell my partner before this because I thought I'd just miscalculated my dates, but looking back over the charts (I have loads of charts), I had not. So, when I told him, we decided to wait a little longer, and then three days later I got a test. We did the test the next morning, and there was a teeny tiny faint pink line. A little part of me was so incredibly excited by this, but I tried my hardest to play it down. Why? Because I knew I was going to have problems and I don't know, I just didn't feel like it was real, and believe me, I so so badly wanted it to be real. We had discussed when we would tell our parents, and went through the "holy fucking shit what if we are really actually going to do this?" moments a couple of times. It was exciting, thrilling, and utterly terrifying. Then, the day after we did the test, I had really REALLY bad stomach pains. Worse than any pain you could possibly imagine. I felt sick, dizzy, and just awful. Then Aunt Flo decided to show up, but this was unlike anything I had ever experienced before. Sure, my periods are bad at times, but I've never had to take time off work for them, and I've never been physically sick because of it. There was so much blood. Clotting. The cramps made me dizzy and sick. Then came the emotions. I cried so much. I cried silently in the toilets at work, I cried driving to and from work, I cried in the shower, but never in front of anyone. I didn't want anyone to know what was going on, because I cannot face the awkward sympathetic look on people's faces when you tell them something like that - how do you even do that?

 I didn't want to cry in front of my love, because I didn't want him to see how upset I was. It was the most horrific experience I have ever been through. On the surface, I was just Hollie, going on as normal. I tried to push it to the back of my mind and throw myself into work, because the other option was grieving, which made me feel like a failure, and trust me, I already feel like that most of the time. On the inside my world was crumbling. I felt empty. The weekend came and went with a blur, and I tried my hardest to cover up the feelings of loss and the pain. I tried to put on a brave face, whatever that is, to mask my disappointment from my partner, and just wanted this feeling of loss to be over.

On the Monday lunchtime, I went to the doctors, and they confirmed to me that I was no longer pregnant and had probably experienced what they so lovingly call a chemical pregnancy. I don't really remember much of what they had said to me, it was all so matter of fact at the time, I just couldn't really take it in. I was given pain relief, and sent home. It was such a surreal experience to go through. The second time it happened a couple of months later, I knew the signs, so I didn't feel the need to go to the doctors, so I didn't. I stayed home and hugged a hot water bottle and waited for it to pass, because that's all I could do. Crying over it doesn't really seem like an option. I just had to keep telling myself "It was hardly even a ball of cells. It wasn't anything".

It's horrible to even write that down, because to me it was something. Now I'm terrified every time my period is a couple of days late that I'm going to go through the whole thing again. That's the joy of the infertility train. your emotions go more haywire than usual. You don't allow yourself to think happy thoughts because it's all been taken away from you so many times, you don't feel like there is much point. If anything positive comes from this, it's that it has given me a much thicker skin. The downside is that it put my anxiety into overload and I am a 24/7 nervous wreck.

Obviously, there are others out there who have been through far far worse than I have. But because we don't talk about it, women feel ashamed to tell people, and it makes it so hard to break down the barriers. I've heard from so many women that they experienced miscarriage, some more than once. Some much further along than 12 weeks, which is deemed the "safe window" once you have the 12 week scan. This is such a delicate subject, so we need to discuss it more. With the help of the Miscarriage Association, hopefully this chapter will help.

(on a side note, if you have suffered from a miscarriage and need to speak to someone, if you need advice, support, comfort, facts, please contact the Miscarriage Association. They are an incredible charity and they do the most amazing work for women who have gone through this awful experience. You'll find their details at the back of this book)

"One day I noticed a bit of a pale brownish pink stain on the toilet paper when I went to the loo, and I wasn't sure why, but I didn't worry. I just assumed it was something normal and pregnancy related, and didn't give it any more thought. I noticed it more regularly over the next few weeks, but again, I naively put it down to being a normal pregnancy thing, and didn't concern myself with it.
At that time, I had never even thought about miscarriage or anything going wrong, it didn't enter my head. When I was 13 weeks into my pregnancy, we went for our first scan at our local NHS hospital. We had both taken that week off work as annual leave so we could relax and celebrate once we had our scan pics, enjoy showing our family and bathing in the happy glow. After a few minutes into the scan, there were some worried looks exchanged and the sonographer going to get someone else to have a look. We kind of guessed this probably wasn't how it should be and alarm set in. They told us that unfortunately the baby had stopped developing at around 8 weeks 5 days and that there was no heartbeat. They asked me if I'd had any idea, any bleeding or pain, and I said no – genuinely not thinking at the time of the slight pinkish discharge I'd had."

There is one thing I have to tell you in this chapter and this is very important. This is for anyone who is pregnant, who has had a miscarriage, or is worried. The loss of a life, no matter how great or small, no matter if that life was four weeks old or fourteen weeks old, affects everyone in different ways. It is not your fault that this has happened and you are not to blame. Miscarriage is a frightening, upsetting and truly traumatising experience for anyone who experiences it. Of that there is no doubt. It is unique to everyone as to how they will go through this process.

The experience of pregnancy loss is different for everyone. What the loss of your baby means to you, and how you feel about it, will be shaped by all kinds of things to do with the person you are and your circumstances. So, although you may find you share a lot with others, it's important to remember that no one else's experience of miscarriage will be exactly like yours. The Miscarriage Association have helped to ensure that everything I write in this chapter is accurate. I hope that it does not take anything away from the brave women who have been through this dark time. They have courageously made it through to the light at the other end of the tunnel.

Miscarriage is the most common type of pregnancy loss, affecting around one in four pregnancies. It can affect any woman, regardless of if she is of picture perfect health or not. A lot of women will experience a very early miscarriage at some point in their lifetime, sometimes, you don't even know it has happened. This can be more commonly called a chemical pregnancy. This is when your pregnancy is so early that it cannot be defined as anything more than a blastocyst at this point. That doesn't make the loss any more significant though, take it from me.

The way miscarriages are described in TV and movies is very over dramatic. You might notice you are passing a little blood, and having some pain in your lower stomach, kind of like period pains but more prominent. You'll probably have a much heavier type period than usual, but there won't be a pool of blood surrounding you if it is an early miscarriage. If you are having an ectopic pregnancy, you will have sharper pains in your stomach and back.

Migraines are not uncommon, but regardless, if you are concerned, just go to your GP. Ectopic pregnancies can be fatal if they do not get picked up early and can cause you even more problems later along the line. Unfortunately, and most heart-breaking of all, some women have no symptoms at all. Many discover that their pregnancy has ended only when they have a routine ultrasound scan at 12 weeks.

Not much is known about the reasons why women will have a miscarriage. It varies so much from person to person and more often than not there is no reason known why it can happen. It can be anything from a chromosomal defect, sporadic, one off defects with the sperm or eggs, or the egg may just not have developed properly.

What I can tell you, is that it is very very VERY rarely something you have done or not done. This is especially important if you, like me, have been sat on the back seat of the infertility bus for the last 10 years. Silently waiting and hoping that when it all happens, it all goes smoothly. There is so much stacked against you as it is, and your emotions are constantly on edge already. Because when it doesn't go as well as you would expect, it feels like your body is trying to punish you for something you have done, or not done. Feelings like "should I not run or exercise while I'm in my 2-week window" or "maybe I shouldn't stay up so late". "Should I start taking folic acid". Other ideas creep in like "maybe I should have stopped the caffeine". You end up wasting so much time and effort and energy, Willing for time to stand still while you get a positive.

Then waiting to get to the 12 weeks and it still be positive, and in that time, knowing and feeling like you are walking on a knife edge. You sit and wait for something to go wrong. It's like being handed a lottery ticket, knowing the odds of winning there and then first time around are slim. Then someone sets fire to it and you're still trying to be optimistic that you will win £5.

But I'm getting off the subject here. What I'm trying to tell you, is that you cannot, you absolutely cannot blame yourself for something you have no control over. Yes, nourish and look after your body, look after your mind and soul and most importantly be kind to yourself, but then I don't need to tell you that. But don't blame yourself when something goes wrong and you can't control it. It will be OK. I promise.

"They told us that unfortunately the baby had stopped developing at around 8 weeks 5 days and that there was no heartbeat. They asked me if I'd had any idea, any bleeding or pain, and I said no – genuinely not thinking at the time of the slight pinkish discharge I'd had.

We were taken into a little side room and a midwife came to speak to us to tell us what would happen next. She arranged for me to go into hospital the next day and have a ERPC. (This is being induced to give birth to your baby. Lovingly known as evacuation of retained products of conception. The MA is working with leading groups across the UK to have this wording removed from hospitals.)

She then swiftly took my Bounty pack off me. Bizarrely that was what really got to me at the time – the way she said, 'Oh you'll not be needing that then' and took it away to give to someone else who was going to have a baby."

"When we went into the hospital the next morning, I was a bit miffed to find they put me in a ward with other women who were heavily pregnant. I'm talking clearly near their due dates. Talk about rubbing my face in it. I had to sit and listen to them moaning about problems they were having and I felt like screaming at them that at least they were having their babies. Watching them all going about with their big bumps was horrible. I felt it was quite insensitive, but I guess it's a case of where there is room.

There was a lot of waiting about and form filling-in to do. People came and went, asking me to sign forms for this and consent forms for that. I was handed a form to sign. When I actually read what I was signing, saw that there was a bit that said, 'Reason for procedure', and someone had written in 'unwanted pregnancy'. I couldn't believe it, and I said, 'That's not right, I had a missed miscarriage'. The person scuttled away apologetically and said they would get it rectified, and they came back later with the same piece of paper, but someone had put a line through the 'unwanted pregnancy' bit and written in 'missed miscarriage' next to it instead. Not exactly a great start. Because I was so dazed and upset, I couldn't be bothered complaining. I had the procedure and was getting ready to go home when I was told I needed an anti D injection in case of future pregnancies. A very brisk, matter-of-fact nurse injected it into my bum cheek and it was bloody sore – it truly felt like the final insult and a fitting end to a terrible day! I was a bit of a state after that..."

If you should find yourself going through this situation, I am so truly sorry. This chapter has been so hard for me to put into words. The heart wrenching pain you go through, but it is important that you know what happens in this situation.

If you've had fertility treatment, there is a higher chance that you might have a miscarriage. That's not because of the treatment itself, but because women who've had fertility treatment are often older. That increases the chance of miscarriage. Some fertility problems can also increase the risk of miscarriage, such as PCOS and Endometriosis. Women who have fertility treatment often know they are pregnant very early on, so they will be more aware than most if they have an early miscarriage. You're basically waking up every day in fear thinking that it could be the day that it is all taken away from you, and then the wave of relief that it hasn't. Talk about exhausting.

As you read above in K's experience and my own, it depends on the time of your miscarriage how things are attended to. If you have a miscarriage before 6 weeks, you might not even notice it unless you have had a positive pregnancy test. If and when it happens, please ensure you go to see a nurse or your GP as soon as possible to ensure there aren't any underlying problems and to discuss your options for moving forward. If you find out at your 12-week scan, you will probably (and unfortunately) know the signs. The scan will be stopped and a doctor will be brought in to confirm that a miscarriage has taken place. Your ultrasound will confirm either of the following in this circumstance:

- A complete miscarriage. The pregnancy has miscarried. There may still be a small amount of tissue or blood in the uterus.

- A non-viable pregnancy. This means a pregnancy that hasn't survived but hasn't yet miscarried. You may hear this described in one of the following ways:

- Missed miscarriage (also called silent or delayed miscarriage, or early embryonic demise). This is where the baby has died or failed to develop but your body has not miscarried him or her. The scan picture shows a pregnancy sac with a baby (or foetus or embryo as they will more likely be referred to by the sonographer) inside. But there is no heartbeat and the pregnancy looks smaller than it should be at this stage. You may have had little or no sign that anything was wrong and you may still feel pregnant.

- Blighted ovum or anembryonic pregnancy (which means a pregnancy without an embryo). This is a rather old-fashioned way of describing a missed miscarriage. The scan picture usually shows an empty pregnancy sac.

- Incomplete miscarriage. The process of miscarriage has started but there is still pregnancy tissue in the uterus (womb) and you may still have pain and heavy bleeding.

In all of these situations, the pregnancy will fully miscarry with time, but there are several ways of managing the process. You may be offered a choice, or the hospital might make a recommendation. In most cases you should be able to have time to think about what you can best cope with. It is up to you at the end of the day, to determine how you wish for your miscarriage to be managed. Unless there is a very viable threat to your wellbeing, in which case a doctor will make the call for you. Some of the options that may be offered to you are:

- *Surgically: an operation, usually called Surgical Management of Miscarriage, or SMM. This is an operation to remove the remains of your pregnancy and it is usually done under general anaesthetic. For many years, surgical management of miscarriage was called ERPC, an abbreviation for Evacuation of Retained Products of Conception. This means the removal of the remains of the pregnancy and surrounding tissue. Many people find this term distressing, which is why it should not be used any more in my and many others opinion, but it's possible that you will still hear it or see it written.*

- *Medically: with medication to begin the process of miscarriage. If your baby has died after about 14 or 15 weeks, you are most likely to be managed medically. This is when pills are administered to "kick-start" the process of a delayed or missed miscarriage. Some women experience quite severe abdominal cramps as well as heavy bleeding with this option, but they may prefer this to an operation.*

- *Naturally: letting nature take its course. Some women prefer to wait and let the miscarriage happen naturally. Hospitals may recommend this too, especially in the first three months of pregnancy.*

It can be difficult to know what to expect and when. It may take days or weeks before the miscarriage begins. Most women will experience abdominal cramps, possibly quite severe, and pass blood clots as well as blood.

It may offer some comfort to you to know that in a recent, large research study comparing surgical, medical and natural methods, the study came to three very important conclusions:

- *The risks of infection or other harm are very small with all three methods*
- *Your chances of having a healthy pregnancy in the future are just as good whichever method you choose*
- *Women interviewed for the research study generally coped better when they were given clear information, good support and were able to choose the management method that they felt they could best cope with.*

The MA provided me with the information above but you can read more detail and some personal experiences in their leaflet "Management of a miscarriage". It contains more information regarding miscarriage in the later stages of pregnancy and ectopic pregnancy.

This is where things really baffle me and once again is an area where women are really let down by our healthcare. If you must return to the hospital to have a procedure there is no area as such put aside for women who have suffered a loss.

Every single woman I have spoken to told me about the agonising pain of having to sit in the same waiting area as women at different stages of pregnancy. Why is this a thing? Why is there not a separate waiting room? It doesn't have to be big, but it's really fucking cruel. Why do we sit women who are there to have a surgical procedure to remove the remains of their pregnancy from their bodies in the same room as pregnant women? I also feel that people's attitudes, both in and outside of the medical profession need to be more mindful of women in this situation, and with infertility. (hence me writing this).

The comments we have to take while going through this are bad enough, but some of the comments I have heard from nurses was truly insensitive. I completely understand that as a medical professional, you can't take your work home with you.

This might mean you cannot become emotionally compromised (a la Spock of Star Trek) as this can cause you problems. But a little compassion and a little empathy goes a long way. A cup of tea, a tissue and a quiet moment to collect your thoughts isn't much to ask, but will go a long way and make someone feel a little better in this absolute minefield of a scenario.

This is where the Miscarriage Association comes in. They work with health professionals to promote more sensitive care, and clearer information on our choices when in this situation. Ruth Bender Atik, Director, says, "when you are looking after someone who has suffered a miscarriage, kindness, compassion and clear information are key and can really help in the most difficult times." The language and terminology referenced with terminations and miscarriages needs to change too. Evacuation of Retained Products of Conception? Really? Calling A miscarriage an Embryo, not a Baby? I'm a pro-choice woman all the way and can understand people think that disassociating the word BABY makes things easier but in this case, it really doesn't.

It's the smallest things that can make the biggest difference. These small changes can make things just that little bit easier when you are faced with this terrible time.

You are more than entitled to take a few days to come to terms with what has happened. This is an extremely emotional and distressing time for you to go through, and more than ever you will need the support of your partner and loved ones. This is going to be extremely emotional to discuss with those around you and this next subject matter is dedicated to them. If you are finding it hard to speak to people about what has happened, maybe show them this chapter. I wrote this to myself when I went through it the first time, and didn't ever show it to anyone. For me, it was more about what I would say if I had to. I didn't want to go around shouting it from the rooftops (can you blame me?)

"I've had a miscarriage and I don't want people to feel sorry for me. I found out that I had miscarried at 6 weeks, and have had it confirmed by my GP. I haven't told anyone what happened, because there was no point. It was nothing, but it still hurts. I feel very emotional right now. There are babies everywhere and I just want them to all go away for just 5 minutes so I can have some baby free grieving time to get over what has happened.

I feel empty even though there was barely anything there. Everywhere I look I see babies and bumps and it hurts so much, but I don't want to and I refuse to cry about this on the outside. I want to just move on. I have cried about this, I have cried uncontrollably in toilets, in bed, in the shower, when I've been out running. I have had dreams reliving what happened to me, and dreams where it didn't happen and we had a baby. I'm a bit confused right now. I don't know how to tell my love that this has happened. I just told him that Aunt Flo has dropped in. I don't think either of us really wants to think about the other option, which is the one that did happen. I'm not going to take any time off work though. I just want to move on with things. I don't think they would do much about it anyway, and besides, I don't really want them knowing, it's no one's business but mine. Ours. well, mine, because I haven't told him.

I haven't told any of my friends, because I don't want them to think I'm being over dramatic or overreacting, I mean, at 6 weeks, it's nothing, it's barely cells. There is no heartbeat, no nothing. But they were my cells. We made them, and they tried to live in my body and for some reason that didn't happen. I hate my body right now. This is the one thing I am supposed to do as a human being, to procreate, and I can't do it. What if I did tell him and he realizes how hard it is going to be and decides he wants out, like everyone else? I just can't take this sort of feeling any more. Enough of that Hollie, you can't think like this. You should man up. This is what happens to one in four people. So, you need to get over it and get on with it. Your time will come. Just stay positive, keep an open mind on things, and it will all be fine. I promise"

Talking about miscarriage is tough. It's a really fucking hard conversation to have with anyone. Weather it's your family, your partner, your friends, it's completely up to you as to who you tell, how much you tell them, and you are quite within your rights to not tell anyone if you don't want to. But we need to talk about it. Because if we don't, those one in four who do miscarry won't ever have a voice.

I'm not saying you need to go and announce it to the world the day you find out, but it will do you and your partner (and your sanity) good to talk to someone about this. A family member you are both comfortable confiding in, a support group, or your fertility clinics Councillor. The Miscarriage Association offers support, guidance and advice, and will be able to help connect you with a counsellor if you need one via their website. If you don't want to vocalize your thoughts and feelings, write things down. Try to practice it in front of a mirror.

Most importantly, remember that when you do tell people it's going to be really hard for them to take in too. They might come out with some comments that you don't want to hear, they might not say anything at all. It's hard for them to take in. It's hard for anyone to take. Don't shut them out, and don't bottle up the emotions you have.

I'm not saying you have to tell the world, but as I've said all throughout this, speaking to someone you can trust will help you get through it. You will be surprised that even though you feel so completely alone right now, there will be other people you know that have been through what you are going through. If you want to tell people via a blog or social media, prepare to be amazed at the amount of people who will message you and tell you that either they or someone they know has been through this experience. Don't believe me? These are some of the messages I got when I first published my blog (now known as chapter one):

"I suffered a miscarriage last August at 8 weeks and it was horrific! Only 1 week after I lost that pregnancy I somehow miraculously fell pregnant again and here she now is. You are incredibly brave for speaking up. I felt very alone and only wish that more women would talk about their experiences. It doesn't make it easier but it's comforting to know you didn't do anything wrong"

"I know it's very different for me already having my little one but after 3 miscarriages I worry that I won't be able to give my boyfriend of a year a child. I always get asked when I'm going to give my daughter a brother or sister. If only it was that easy."

"I also had an early miscarriage and it was one of the most upsetting, soul destroying things ever. And every day of this pregnancy I am checking for blood and praying that I don't find any."

My friend, H's comment, about already having children really struck a chord. Even though you may already have a child, it doesn't mean that the trauma of going through the trying to conceive period is any easier. The heartbreak of miscarriage is still there. It's no different at ally.

To every woman out there who has been through this, you are amazing,

Thank you to Ruth and Lisa from the Miscarriage Association for their help with this difficult chapter; I'd be lying to you all if I didn't tell you that I have cried while I write this.

Act Eight - From the outside looking in

So, I don't want this to come off as me just whinging, which was my biggest worry with this. I have this friend. She's my best friend in the whole world. We have known each other since we were 12 years old and sat next to one another on our first day at high school. We got through those awkward teenage years together. We supported each other through university, first jobs, and even when there was 600 miles between us, we still supported one another.

Cut to the present day, my best friend is married, and had her first baby in 2016 who is completely gorgeous. We got to meet her 2 months into her time on this planet and she melted my heart. As we sat there on the sofa, talking about little miss E and how gorgeous she is, my friend told me how much it infuriated her that people would ask her if her baby was an accident or planned. I totally get it, because it's very personal and no one needs to know that apart from you, the parents. I asked her, and she told me she was planned, and then apologized, because they didn't have to try for very long. I asked her "why are you apologizing?!" she told me in so many words that she didn't want to upset me. Now, I totally appreciate this and anyone in my situation would, but by this point, it's irrelevant. My feelings of jealously and upset have completely disappeared. I'm so happy for her.

I never want my friends to feel like they can't talk to me about things that bring them complete and utter happiness. It made me realize that we didn't really talk a lot during her early pregnancy and I'm not sure if that was deliberate on my part, her part or both? I would sometimes see her baby bump photos and announcements and felt that pang of jealously. I hated myself for thinking "I wish people would just give it a rest, we don't need a monthly update". But she wasn't doing anything that new parents or expecting parents do, she was happy, so why couldn't I be happy for her? And has it had an impact on our friendship? I really hope not. That day when we talked about everything, I told her not to feel like she can't talk to me about these things. I just want to be asked how I am occasionally.

I thought it was important to include how it feels to be on the other side of the fence. She's my best friend in the world, and when you are going through all of this, you must keep these precious friends close.

"When those lines turned blue on the pregnancy test my heart sang with joy. My husband and I spoke about how we would announce it to our parents and then our friends. Of course, our parents were over the moon when we told them the news in only week six of my pregnancy. We then had the long wait until our first scan at twelve weeks. Once that came, we were then able to go public with our news.

This was more difficult than I imagined it to be. I wanted to shout my news from the rooftops and I wanted everyone to be overjoyed for us. However, having a friend who is struggling to conceive suddenly makes you stop and think. This isn't just any friend either, this was my best friend. I was scared Hollie would feel hurt, jealous or angry. Would I lose my friend of over ten years? Hollie has always been so happy for my husband and me. She always expressed her happiness at our future, with children in it. Did I remember this when announcing my pregnancy though? No, I didn't. Fear of upsetting Hollie took over and I didn't tell her our good news. I wanted to, believe me. I did the cowardly thing and announced it through Facebook. Of course, Hollie, the beautiful person that she is, congratulated us immediately. I will never make that mistake again. Thankfully I have a very forgiving friend.

All was well throughout my pregnancy. Hollie sent me messages regularly, checking my health and wellbeing. A friend I could always rely on. We discussed her want to conceive and how hard it was for her and her partner. It was heart-breaking to hear. There I was in my pregnancy bubble whilst she was exploring ways to get to that stage. It made me sad that such kind people, who had so much love to give, couldn't share that love with a baby of their own.

When my beautiful baby girl was eventually born, Hollie arranged a visit to come meet her. I was excited, as I always am about her visits. We arranged the visit a few weeks in advance, but as it got closer the nerves started to kick in again. I spoke to my husband about my anxieties over Hollie's emotions. Will she break down in tears when she sees her? Will she deny her existence? Yes, very stupid questions I know, but I'm not always the most rational of people! When Hollie and her partner turned up, it was wonderful. No awkwardness, no ignoring my baby. Just two people, full of love for my child.

When my husband and Hollie's partner popped to the shops, we had THE conversation. I had questions for Hollie. I wanted to know how she was feeling, how her fertility journey was going and quite simply, was she OK? The bottom line is, she's my best friend and this can't be easy for her and I wanted her to know that I could be her shoulder to cry on. Hollie amazed me with her strength whilst talking about her tribulations. She told me the long process she was going to have to go through. The intrusive procedures, the tests, the analysis. It exhausted me just hearing about it, but it also told me the lengths they would go to to have a child.

Reading extracts of this book throughout the process, I can see the pain, heartache and longing that Hollie has poured into every page, every word. There is nothing she wants more now than to be a mummy and I get that. Yes, I've had my child and was one of the lucky ones not to struggle to conceive, but I still get it. Now I have my baby, I understand that there is nothing better. I know that someone like Hollie deserves the chance to feel the way I get to feel when I look at my daughter. I hope that one day, in the not so distant future, I'm able to congratulate my best friend on her pregnancy and be there for her like she was for me.

To my best friend Hollie, I am so proud of you. I will always be here for you and I will do anything to help you get what you want so badly on every step of your journey."

I've mentioned a couple of times my lovely partner. He truly is a delight, and I can honestly put my hand on my heart and say he has made me so happy and I absolutely adore him. When we first met on our first date I told him in my slightly intoxicated state that I might not be able to have children. I felt it was important to be upfront with him, because he had been upfront with me about his past and that he wanted kids - who was I to lie to him or deceive him? Luckily, his response was "well, we will just have to try extra hard then" and that was basically the end of the subject! Fast forward to today, over a year and a half later, and nothing has really changed. We are starting to get our investigation tests done, and I think because we know it's going to take a while that makes things a little easier for us. But sometimes, I get this feeling, and I am sure U can't be alone in this, that it must just be a giant pain in the arse for him to have to go through all this. I mean, on that first date he could've just said "you know what, this isn't going to work then" and gone on to date someone whose reproductive system is completely fine. I worry about this, and I think that it is something that is a valid worry for me. What if he can't be bothered with all this stuff and calls it quits?

I asked him to write a piece into this book, not for me, but for other couples in our situation who might be faced with the same feelings that we have.

"At the time of writing, Hollie and I have been dating for over two years, and for most of that time we've been living together. This relationship certainly moved quickly and we are just fine with that - sometimes things just feel right. Living together wasn't the only thing in this relationship that happened quickly, maybe quicker than convention asserts.

We've already started trying for children.

Now, if you've read this far, then I'm pretty sure you can understand why we have taken the step a lot quicker than others. For reasons out of our control, it makes sense to start this sooner rather than later. So, before I talk more about that decision I will go a bit further back in time.

Before meeting Hollie, I had been previously been married. At the time I didn't think it, but I would probably say now that marrying at 26, I was too young. Even at that point you change so much growing further into adulthood, which is what happened to me. We'd married with the idea of starting a family at some point, as most couples do, but as we changed and grew our plans for the future no longer aligned, that's all I'll say about that. In truth, separating was the best thing for us anyway and gave us both a chance to go back into the big bad world, start again and enjoy new experiences.

I struggled with the idea of suddenly being single again. I come from a loving family, my brother is my best friend and I love my parents dearly. For me, family has always been the most important thing and I can't imagine a future without children.

On our first date, Hollie told me that for her, conceiving might be difficult. I don't know whether it was the beers talking (Dutch courage, it was a first date!) or my natural sense of "I can do anything", but I told her that wasn't a problem - hey, I like a challenge. At that time, I still wasn't even thinking about children for another few years anyway, let's cross that bridge when we come to it. Of course, we came to it far sooner than expected when the reality of it all set in.

I think I can be forgiven for being nervous about what the future holds, but then, aren't we all? Life doesn't always take you down the easiest path, or the path you want. When I was a kid, I wanted to be a vet. As a teenager, I wanted to be a pilot. In my 20's, I wanted to be a Rockstar. In my 30's, I want to be an astronaut. All throughout, I've wanted to be a parent. Did I picture myself one day doing the job of my dreams, (which I pretty much have, though it's not as an astronaut) in a nice house, (that's in the pipeline) with my awesome other half (nailed it) and our perfectly behaved children? Did you? Doesn't everyone?

Life throws up all sorts of twists and turns and all we can do is face each challenge and do our best. I know I've got a strong woman by my side and whatever comes our way, we'll go through together, as a team.

So yes, we're trying for children. If it happens tomorrow, then wow. It's soon and it will be scary but it will be amazing and we'll face it. The truth is, it's likely to not happen and it's likely that we'll need to go down the IVF route. That means that thanks to the NHS, time is against us. A few months ago, I sat in a fertility support group listening to the testimonies of a variety of couples. Seeing a 38-year-old woman break down because IVF would not be available to her was heart-breaking. She can't afford her own treatment and that means she'll most likely never have children. Procreation isn't just a human right, it's the very essence of life. It's the point of life, right?

The next step was for me to get checked. Not much scares me and not much makes me nervous. The process itself didn't bother me (Chaps - I know the idea of taking that cup and walking into the room might seem a little embarrassing, but the staff in those places are professional, for once in your life you're just a number - embrace that.) Waiting for those test results was almost hellish. I kept imagining that I would be told that I was infertile, that I could never have children of my own, and that thought really affected me. In those few weeks, I became quite a dark person, trapped in the idea of something I had no control over. I wondered what I would do, where I would go, how I would react. In truth, it kind of scared me. It made me think "How do people cope with this?"

The results came and I was one of the lucky ones. Aside from a few little anomalies, I was OK. That increases our chances, but it also made me feel quite guilty for Hollie's sake. Knowing that she didn't get that good news about her own health made me realize just how lucky I am. I can't imagine what it must feel like to get that bad news there.

Guys and girls, I feel for you, I really do.

What all this has made me do is to consider things and realize that there are options, and that being a parent is more than just genes. If someone told me tomorrow that my Dad wasn't my 'real Dad', I would tell them he is.

Being a parent is more than just genes and that means it's the one life goal that will come true. It's not going to be easy, but knowing that I am doing it with someone who wants it just as much as I do means more to me than anything. we will do whatever it takes to make that dream a reality"

Knowing someone who is experiencing the turmoils of infertility is daunting. But if you have friends or a partner who has confided in you about this then honestly you must be a pretty damn awesome person yourself. I am so grateful for my friends and to my amazing partner for sticking with me throughout all this and beyond.

Act Nine - What happens when you stop trying?

For the larger number of couples who seek infertility treatment, it will be successful. Some may not need as much as others, it might happen straight away. Some may go through treatment for years, which in turn feel like a lifetime in themselves. Around three quarters of couples who undergo treatment in some form, whether it be clomid or IVF, whether it take 6 months or 6 years, it will be a success.

But what about the rest? And when do you throw in the towel and make that decision to stop trying, and decide to move on from that dream of having a family by this means?

Making the decision to undergo fertility treatment is a difficult one, and is one of the hardest decisions to make. It may seem pretty simple for someone who hasn't had to make that sort of call - you get sick, you go to the doctor, your car breaks down, you take it to a mechanic. But infertility isn't specifically an illness (except for things like PCOS and endometriosis). You're not going to die as a result of it, it isn't a threat to your wellbeing. It carries no symptoms other than the emotional ones that you feel. But we still have to make that decision of when to ask for help, and by help, I mean medical intervention.

But what if you go through all of that and it still doesn't work?
The standard knee jerk reaction from a lot of people who aren't in your shoes and don't have to make the decision themselves is usually something along the lines of "you can always adopt? Have you thought about fostering?" or something like that. For some, this is an option that can give them the family they have dreamed of for so long, and is a compellingly rewarding and beautiful thing for many childless couples to do. But it's not for everyone. So, stop recommending it like it's some amazing cure, please? We don't appreciate it.

Experts recommend that women wrestling with the decision to stop fertility treatments look at their loss as they would any other.

"The person has to go through a process of mourning for what this was going to be in their life and who they were going to be in this life," said Mardy S. Ireland, a psychoanalyst from Berkeley, California, who specializes in childlessness.

Infertility treatment can be so all-consuming that many women keep trying long after the odds become prohibitive. Those who learn to accept that no treatment in the world will allow them to become pregnant have the best chance of learning to accept a childless life.

For many couples, the pain never really goes away. Like a niggling pain in your spine, it's always there, lingering in the background. Every now and again it flares up, either through an involuntary irritation (such as an insensitive relative at a family gathering piping up with "still no kids then? Better get another pet! That happened people - why don't aunts and uncles come with a filter?) or a stabbing pain, such as meeting your friends beautiful baby for the first time.

Making the decision to stop all the invasive, uncomfortable treatments and deciding that enough is enough can be the makings of a couple. If you have been through all this together, the heartbreak, the pain (both physical and emotional), then you are in a very special and beautiful place. But the important thing here is to remember that having a child does not define you. In the very same way, not having a child does not make you any less of a person, or a couple. You are not defined by your offspring, or indeed, your ability to produce any. But the content of your character, your soul, and your own personality and kindness, they are what makes you you. You should never allow your journey, no matter what stop you get off the infertility bus at, define your final destination.

Talking to your partner about when to stop treatments is something you should discuss, ideally before you even start. Knowing what your limits are as a couple will help you to come to terms with what you are going to put yourselves and your relationship through. The most important thing here is that you agree when you both will want to stop. It can't be one or the other, you need to be in this together - teamwork makes the dream work, right?

In some cases, the decision will be made for you. A medical complication may mean it isn't possible for you to have any more treatments. You will then have to look at other options, maybe these will include surrogacy or adoption. This can be anything from cancer to fibrosis, or indeed, a complication may arise during your treatment.

Complications such as ovarian hyperstimulation will halt treatment until your body decides to behave itself. for some, that just doesn't happen. It could be that you or your partner has a medical condition that if passed on could cause you and your baby health problems, such as HIV, AIDS. Or even a hereditary condition that could in turn cause health defects in your unborn baby. In these cases, fertility treatment may be stopped or indeed not even begin.

The idea of stopping all the treatment can trigger many different emotions in different people. Many feel relieved that there are no more treatments, no more appointments and no more needles. No more decisions will need to be made. No more fingers crossed when finding out you are pregnant. No more anxious days and weeks, waiting for a scan. No more medical intervention when things go wrong. It can feel like a huge weight has been lifted from your shoulders. You can start to move on and move into a different chapter of your life, whether that be with children by other means or not.

You are more than likely to find that the raw and intense feelings you have will ease over time. That's not to say that there won't be a continuing sadness, especially on dates and occasions, but there can also be some comfort in knowing the stress you have left in another chapter is closed. you may find some relief in closing the door on 'trying' and allow yourself to think about moving on to a different kind of future from the one you had planned.

After making the decision to stop trying for a baby, many people move on with their lives in all sorts of different ways. Some couples consider the different ways of becoming a parent. Others may decide to move on without directly parenting and become more involved with their nephews and nieces or the children of friends. Although this might be painful at times, being part of a child's life can also bring much happiness.

You may choose to build a different life, without a focus on children. Not having children means you might be more flexible in the way you live your life and you can find time and energy for other things. Some people throw themselves into new things that they may not have ever considered before going through treatment. This could be anything from travelling to new places, taking up a new hobby, or taking the plunge and doing something they have always wanted to do but put off in the quest to have children. Closing the door on trying can mean opening another door to other interests and opportunities.

Even if you stop trying, there may still be times when it's difficult to be around other people with children, especially if they seem to be the main topic of conversation. You might find it helps to spend time with other friends and family who don't have children or whose children have grown up. But whatever happens, remember that you are a whole person with or without children. I know many couples who don't have children who are as happy and whose lives are as rich and fulfilled as those friends of mine who have kids. Friends who had the guts to take the plunge, sell everything they own and pack their bags and travel the world. I also know those who have done that and packed a 2-month-old baby in too!

Talking to people who have been faced with the same issues as you can also be helpful. I appreciate I've gone on about the therapy and counselling loads, but it works! The organisation More to Life is an amazing group whose members are childless by circumstance rather than by choice. This online community provides new social opportunities as well as support to other people in the same situation. Some people feel that moving to a new house can help them make a new start. This may be especially true if they live in what was to be a family house which perhaps holds too many sad memories. Like Mr I said in Act 4:

"Early this year we also decided to move home. We had originally lived in the city before moving 40 miles north, to be out of the city life, and it was also so that we could get a house with a garden and be closer to my family. Baby preparation time! That's all fallen through and because of the toll the commute was taking on my wife, we made the decision to move back to town. When the move was becoming a reality, it hit home how gut-wrenching it was that our family plans hadn't come to fruition. It was a happy but sad time all in one. However, now it seems like the best decision we made because we both couldn't be happier living back in the city. We are closer to our friends and in a place where it's a lot easier to do things as the choices are greater."

Above all, in the same way that taking those first steps into fertility treatment, moving on from fertility treatment is a journey in itself. It is one of finding and building a new life and a different sense of identity and purpose. It can be hard to get through that journey and you might find that you and your partner deal with it very differently. Some relationships don't survive this change in direction – but many do and are strengthened by it. What I'm trying to tell you is your life isn't limited to all this fertility stuff. You should live your own life and do things for you every once in a while. Go out, soak up some culture in a different part of the world, sit at home in your pj's, binge watch your favourite TV show until your eyes go funny. Drink (good) wine. Eat great food. Sit up all night with your nearest and dearest and solve all life's problems. Run marathons, watch movie marathons. See the world, and above all do things that make YOU happy. You can't put your life on hold because of infertility. You are more than it.

K was one of the few people I spoke to about moving on from infertility. Her account of the grief that she felt about not being able to give her daughter a sibling and how she moved on from wanting another child is inspired. I hope that it will help others know that even after 7 years your life can go on.

"After almost another year, I realized one day when I got up and got my period, that I had no idea what cycle day I was on. I hadn't even been thinking about getting my period, and getting pregnant hadn't actually been at the forefront of my mind at all lately. I wasn't even that bothered about getting my period. I just went 'huh, ok', and got on with my day without giving it another thought. I guess I had just been getting on with other things.

Perhaps my brain was actually getting used to NOT thinking about getting pregnant all the time, like a reverse of what had happened to get me into this state? I think I had gotten used to the idea that, my life is pretty cool as it is, and I am quite content. I have a wonderful family, a husband who loves me - warts and all. I have a gorgeous girl, I have my health, my pets, my parents, a cosy home, a job I don't mind...the list goes on. What I also have now is perspective. I have watched friends that I was previously jealous of experience bad things; marriages breaking up, deaths, majorly stressful situations. I won't get this time back ever again, and I'm not going to waste another moment of my life. I've waited long enough. It's now 7 years since we embarked on trying for that elusive second child, and I'm in a much better place.

It's not the be-all and end-all I once thought it was. I still have the odd pang, and the odd blip, I guess that's only natural. You can't just turn off your feelings totally. Interestingly, my period was almost a week late recently, and for a few days there I started walking around, letting those sneaky little exciting thoughts creep in. What if...just what if...a little smile crept across my face and I started picturing my life with this late, unexpected baby.

Buying buggies and all the paraphernalia that comes with them, walking my dog with the baby in a buggy. Working out how old it would be when my daughter starts high school...hmm...but then BANG! Back to reality with a bump as I wake up to that all too familiar cramping feeling and my period comes and normal sensible service is resumed. Oh well. It was nice to dream for a bit...very nice!

I kind of feel I've come full circle with all this stuff. I've certainly been through the wringer with it and experienced a wealth of emotions and feelings I never would have dreamt of. I had to wade through the bad stuff and come out the other side to get to where I am now. For me, it took as long as it took. It was a gradual acceptance and understanding of my circumstances, and my feelings, mixed with a real effort to try and change things for the better.

Now I'm facing 40 and I'm finally finding my feet in this world, what's next? Who knows if I will ever have that other child. One thing is for sure – if I do, he or she will be loved immensely and welcomed with open arms (slightly wrinkled arms at this rate!) but I will not waste any more of my precious days worrying about what I know I don't know and those things I can't control. Life is way, way too short."

One of the hardest things about living with infertility is not knowing if you will ever be a parent. You feel so many emotions all the time, this can be too much for some people to bear, for others, it can make them stronger. You may feel positive about continuing to try for a baby, whether you need more treatment. You might just fall pregnant naturally. On the other hand, you may wonder just how long you should keep putting yourself and your partner through this, whether you can cope with the possibility of more disappointment.

Infertility is such a rollercoaster both physically and mentally. The added heartbreak of miscarriage or it not working at all might make you wonder if you can take any more. You might start thinking about other ways of being a parent, like adoption or fostering. You may decide that you will learn to live without children and move on to a different kind of future.

It's important to know that your feelings are likely to change over time and you might make and 'unmake' these decisions several times. I cannot stress enough how much it helps to have support from your partner and loved ones if you choose to tell them. If you choose not to, counselling, weather in a group or on a one on one basis will provide you will respite and release of your feelings.

You can't bottle up those, otherwise you will eventually explode. Talk about your emotions, drink endless cups of tea in group and individual therapy. It may not sound like much, but it will help you come to terms with the feelings you have and realize you are not alone. Infertility and everything that goes with it is not a solitary sentence, even though I now if can feel like it. You are never alone, and there will be always be someone to talk to if you need them.

Act Ten - In Conclusion

When I started writing this book, I had no idea what it was going to be. It was originally going to be a blog project, because I never really wanted to write a book about it. I still don't think there's enough content here, but the big problem with this is that there simply isn't enough information out there for people to find.

What there is out there is so darn scientific and jargon-ed up that you don't even know where to begin! It's a mind-boggling paradox of wanting all the information you can find, but you don't know what is trustworthy and what is a load of crap. Honestly, some of it is complete and utter nonsense! I hope that someone out there reads this and it sheds a bit of light on what it's like to go through all this. we are still going through will be for a while, and who knows, it might work, it might not. Only time will tell I guess.

The people I feel for more than anything from the research I've done, are the guys out there who are infertile. As a woman, we are slightly better equipped to talk about this sort of thing with other people (we don't do it enough by the way). But guys, seriously, it's 2017, and like I've already said it's OK to moisturize and cry. The guys we met at the support group were so open about what they were going through with one another, I would love it if people could talk about this outside of the haven of the support group. Stigmas suck. And the best way to get rid of them is to break down the barriers and talk about things. If we make the issue a little bit more normal it shouldn't be so hard?

While I'm on the subject, ladies, we gotta talk about what's going on down there a bit more every once in a while. There is no shame at all in talking to your friends about something you are concerned with when it comes to your internal plumbing. we all get a visit from Aunt Flo once a month or so, we know how it works, so why don't we ask questions about it?! I guess society has stuck that particular stigma together.

It made periods a dirty word that shouldn't be talked about openly - fuck society. Fuck those stupid adverts where the panty liners have blue liquid soaked into them, we bleed real blood and that's normal. Periods happen and they suck, but women just get on with it.

If we talked about this more it might make girls who are a little more self-conscious open up about something they're worried about. Maybe go to the doctor and discuss it with them. It could be nothing, but it could also be something, and that something could lead to worse things. Let's talk about it ladies! You only have one body. Take care of it.

Going through all this infertility business is pretty tough, it's frightening and lonely and can make people feel isolated and confused. But the reason people feel isolated is because we don't know how to talk about it, and we don't know how to react when someone tells us they can't have kids. One piece of advice? Don't look at them like they've handed you a dead mouse - that can be the worst, when people ask us "when are you having kids?" and our reply is not something they want to hear, people don't know what to do. We are not dying! so don't make out like we are.

At the same time, if someone tells you that they are going through this and you want to do your best to be there for them all I can say is just be there for them. Please don't try and offer us the advice your mums sisters friend heard on mumsnet, because we've most likely googled it already. Don't ask us if we are going to adopt because we likely haven't considered it yet. And please, PLEASE, don't say things like "it will happen when it's supposed to happen". Or "it's just one of those things that takes time". we know that, and the reason we are going though this is because it's not happening when it's supposed to and it's taken way longer than it should!

Just be an ear for them to vent to and a shoulder to cry on when we need it (that goes for you too guys). If you do have kids, don't act like you can't talk about them to us or share your joy with us. Because we love it when you do that, but don't forget to ask us how we are every now and again. We like to talk about other things than babies and bumps, and I'm sure you do too. Normal stuff will help us take our mind off things.

We need to talk about infertility and all the bells and whistles that go along with it. One in five couples in the UK is going through infertility treatment now. Right now. For those one in five, being handed a card that says, "you are one in five" can have the same psychological effects as being diagnosed with cancer. That sounds weird, because we talk about cancer all the time. We have fund raisers, we have many charities, we have coffee mornings, bake sales, "dryathlons" (the worst thing ever), people who run marathons, all to raise awareness for cancer, and that's great. But for infertility? Not so much.
We talk about it in hushed tones and only with certain people, in fear that people will judge us because of it. We don't have national coffee mornings, you don't see people running the London Marathon in a costume to raise money for infertility (I would love someone to prove me wrong on this by the way). That's because it's not really an illness. But the effects of it can cause you just as much pain. I often wonder if it would have helped me if I had known that fact when I had the news broken to me at the age of 18 that I would struggle to conceive.

Maybe, as I got older, it would have helped confirm some of the feelings I was having. Maybe it would have encouraged me to talk more about how I was feeling and find the support I really needed. That's a lot of maybe to put on one statistic but you get the general picture.

Talking to other all the women and men for this project has helped me gain a lot of insight into infertility and its impact on both sexes. It's not just a woman's thing. It truly is an emotional roller coaster that both sides will go though, full of overwhelming feelings that can exhaust you to the point of tears. It's hard to see women experiencing so much pressure and then all too often try to contain what they are feeling.

The thing I notice the most is that we can be ridiculously tough on ourselves. We try so hard to act like it's not a big deal because we don't want to be seen as small or weak, and we are not any of those things. There is nothing wrong with asking for help and needing support. One intelligent, self-aware woman, who wanted a second baby so her daughter had a sibling, told me that she felt guilty that she couldn't produce another baby. Another lady told me that the She had experienced 3 rounds of IVF and had 2 miscarriages in the past year. The other round didn't work either. I wouldn't say that that was pretty selfless, and extremely taxing for the body and soul. We shouldn't be so hard on ourselves.

We blame ourselves, we put so much pressure on ourselves and our relationships, and we try so darn hard. It is exhausting and we are exhausted, we are confused and emotionally and physically drained. I wish I could take away all the feelings of confusion, the pain, not to mention the disappointment, and replace it. Give back some spontaneity, happiness for the sake of being happy and a bit of the lost romance. I want to tell these beautiful, strong, inspiring women that everything is going to be OK, but I know that sometimes the OK we want is not the OK we get.

It's not easy to take the struggle away and I know there is no magic answer to feeling better, except drinking endless cups of tea and sobbing uncontrollably every now and again. Emotions are real things people! I do know that if you are struggling with infertility and you haven't already, the best advice I can give you is to find someone to talk to. Find a support group or a community you can share and connect with. Don't contain how you are feeling and don't struggle alone, because you are not alone in this. Find a safe space that you feel comfortable enough to be vulnerable, to open up and share how you are feeling.

It is OK that you feel overwhelmed, or angry or confused or however you are feeling right now. Let's face it - Infertility sucks, it's really shitty, but it's not always going to feel like that. sharing what you are experiencing will help you get through this. I have cried every single time I have been to a support group or doctor's appointment, and that's OK. Emotions and feeling vulnerable are OK. Getting it all out in the open is better than bottling things up and pretending like you don't care or that it doesn't matter. It does matter, and your wellbeing matters.

We need to talk about miscarriage too. We need to talk about it for the same reasons that we don't talk about infertility and then some more. People know it happens, but they choose not to acknowledge it in public because it's such a tough and at times a taboo subject. It's a delicate and difficult subject but women need to know that they are not alone.

One in 5 pregnancies end in a miscarriage, and that's heart-breaking. Especially for the woman who is crying her heart out as a doctor tells her that there isn't a heartbeat. The woman who was so happy just days before with her partner making plans for their family and their future. For the husband who is crying to himself in private while his wife tries to put everything behind her because she thinks it will be the best thing to do. Or for the women like me who are so scared every time her period is late and then cries to herself when it does.

It reminds her of the times before when it was late, and she was pregnant, and then she wasn't, and no one can tell her why it happens, it just does. It's an issue that needs a bigger conversation, because it's a big deal. I knew when I shared the first part of this that people would read it and might get in touch. Its human nature to be empathetic. but what I didn't expect was to be inundated with emails and messages from women who poured their hearts out about their own experiences of miscarriage, and how alone they felt.

Without exception, every single person I spoke to shared their feelings of devastation, hopelessness and isolation. Yet when I asked them why they hadn't mentioned it to me or other people before, they said things like: "it wasn't the time or the place" or "I don't like to talk about it". I suspect this is down to fear, which is understandable. Unless you've lost a baby – or been close to someone who has – it's easy to dismiss a miscarriage as something you just need to "get over" – rather like a cough or a cold.

It's hard to talk about losing a baby when you're not sure people will get what you're going through or – worse still – think you're going for the sympathy vote. After my first miscarriage, I simply didn't want to talk about it for fear of seeming like I was overreacting because it was so early. I felt I had no other choice but to suck it up and move on, I didn't really get time to grieve.

The problem is, both the emotional impact and the physical side of miscarriage are still not widely understood. And unless we break down the barriers, it will always be a topic that is known about but not talked about.

The way in which miscarriages are managed needs to be changed. It is heart-breaking enough to be told that you have had a miscarriage. but to then have to go through a medical procedure with such a clinical name, while waiting in a patient area which is usually shared with pregnant women is cruel.

The nurses need to be better equipped to deal with the types of patients they have. I'm not bashing nurses here - what I mean is they need to be more sympathetic, understand that this is an extremely emotional time for people. A separate waiting and recovery area, a sympathetic ear and some more conscientious language would not go amiss. The Miscarriage Association is working on this, but we still have a lot of work to do.

Guys, we need to talk about male factor infertility and stop acting like it is a lack of or loss of a person's masculinity, of man points. Because it isn't! I found out that my partners dad had a low sperm count, but that does not mean I think any less of him or my partner. I know that it can be a genetic present passed down from generation to generation. But we are a team, so regardless of the results of his tests, we will get through this together.

I also met some great guys who have been through the testing and have been told that they are basically infertile, and that doesn't mean they aren't a real man. Those guys who talk about this stuff openly and frankly, have bigger metaphorical balls than you realize. It takes real nuts to talk about that kind of thing, so can we stop acting like a man is defined by that?!

Men and male factor infertility account for half of all infertility issues for the one in five couples who are having treatment. It's not just a women's problem. The great thing is, with all the advances in medicines and treatments, there is almost always a solution. But we don't talk about it enough for it to be a normal thing. guys, I totally get that you're not going to talk about your low sperm count with the lads at the pub. If you want to find other people who have had this problem, google famous people with infertility problems.

There aren't many guys out there who have openly said, "it's me, it's my swimmers", the results tend to be very female orientated. I googled it, and the only ones I found were Gordon Ramsay, Jimmy Fallon, Mark Zuckerberg, and Hugh Jackman - that was on a list of 18 celebrities. The rest were women. I see the problem here. Don't even get me started on how hard it is to find a male infertility charity website. When I googled it, the first result was for guide dogs UK - forgive me if I'm wrong but being blind isn't a side effect of male infertility?

The other problem is that in order to tackle male infertility on the social level and talk about it, it needs to be reflected in the approach the medical community takes. Around half of fertility issues among couples are a result of male factor infertility – yet no one is talking about how we can improve male fertility. Instead, as soon as a sperm problem identified, we recommend IVF.

...ing putting something in and taking ...he has to take a ...he has to go ...roblem, but the ...nts. How do you think ...wing that the ...n? They can't fix the ...down to us ladies to ...pointing fingers at you ...ver done to treat the problem w... ...nd it should be.

The only way we are going to be able to get th... ugh this, and make some sense of it all, is to be more open about it. We need to have these difficult discussions with people and help them realize that if you are told you will need help, there is no shame in asking for it. Crucially, there is nothing wrong with wanting to talk about it. Infertility is a real thing, and it's not something that is researched enough. Neither is there adequate support available for couples who are going through it.

For example, the support group we go to in Southampton is the only one on the south coast. Our Councillor has had people come from Dorset to the group because there isn't anything near them. The way the medical profession approaches infertility and the language that is used doesn't make it any better. It's such a minefield to get through. Although we are always told there is support available, you want to be able to make informed decisions with the information available to you. You want to be able to do so in a way you understand what is happening. You don't want complex medical jargon. You don't want to sit there in silence while the doctor taps away on the computer without telling you anything.

When I first went to the doctor about my problems there was very little discussion. I was advised that there are two blood tests to be done for me and sperm analysis, and that we should remember to "have sex for the sake of having it". I had my blood tests done, and it took me 2 weeks to get the results, which my partner then had to go and pick up from the doctors. They were just "normal". What are you supposed to do with that information? (Book another appointment and push for another opinion).

If it wasn't for the months of research, I'd still be in the dark about all this, and that sucks. It seems GPS often don't know how to discuss this with patients unless they have experience in the area. So, they recommend and offer advice that can be pretty condescending. I wanted to scream at my doctor, because we have sex, we try not to get stressed and we have been doing it for a while and nothing is happening. Hence why I was sat there with her.

The advances we have in medicines today are making great strides. They are finding cures and treatments for the many medical hurdles that can make the infertility journey even more difficult. The introduction of IVf in the 70's means over five million babies have been born worldwide with the help of fertility treatment. Half of those were born in the last six years. The first 'test tube baby', Louise Brown, was born in 1978, by 1990 there had been an estimated 90,000 births resulting from assisted reproductive technology (ART) worldwide.

Jump forward to 2017, there are medical trials going on in Belgium to utilize artificial ovaries for women who don't have any. Scientists are looking at ways to use skin cells to make embryos for couples who can't make their own eggs. There has been introduction of less invasive types of IVF which involves placing the fertilized eggs into a device which is implanted into the womb instead of a laboratory. This means that couples can feel more included in the process and the whole thing is a little less clinical. But to ensure those of us going through infertility treatment feel less like we have been handed a death sentence, we need to break down the barriers, open up a bit more and talk about these things. It's not a crime to be infertile.

I've learned so much in writing this book/project. There is so much out there to consider and things I hadn't even considered when it comes to infertility. All I would want to come from this is for it all to be a little less confusing! I hope that this information helps others realize that although you might feel alone, you are certainly not alone. The amount of people I heard from who had been through this was crazy. People I knew and am really close with, people on the other side of the world. They poured their hearts out and told me how utterly lonely they felt when they went through IVF, miscarriage, being diagnosed with PCOS, finding out they were firing blanks. That's not because they are alone, because we are not alone. it's just we need to change our perspective on the subject.

Acknowledgements and Thanks

I have many people I want to thank for their individual contributions to this book. It would be impossible for me to list every single person, so I have picked out the ones who I hold closest and most dear, and risk missing out someone just as special to this project. As someone who has never done anything like this before, it's been a daunting process, and I have spent more time that is necessary googling everything I can find in infertility, miscarriage and everything else. I have looked at far too many pictures of PCOS, different types of cervix. I needed to delete the phrase cervical mucus from my google history, and read stories that have made me cry to the point of ugliness. Many of the stories shared are not in this book at the request of the women and men who have poured their hearts out, but that doesn't make them any less important.

An enormous thank you goes to my amazing contributors. There are 16 men and women whose stories are included, of all different ages, stages, and circumstances. Every single one of them has trusted me with something so precious to them, a part of their lives that has been so difficult to go through and to get their heads around, and I just hope that the final product does justice to the struggles they have been through. Many of them are still going through right now. They are the bravest and kindest people I know, some closely, others I may never hear from again, but they are all so important to me. I am keeping them anonymous as promised, but they know who they are, and without you, this wouldn't have happened. This echoes to everyone who has commented on my blog posts, messaged me across my social media and emailed me with your stories and your support. It means so much to me and proved my point even more, that as someone faced with infertility you are never alone.

Huge thanks to The Miscarriage Association, The Fertility Network, Endometriosis trust, IVF Babble and our awesome Councillor at Complete Care Fertility Clinic. Thanks for allowing me to spend way too long on your websites, reading all the leaflets and booklets to get information I needed. It's because of these charities and support networks that women like me can find information that we know we can trust.

The amazing couples we have met at our infertility support group. They have shared stories at our infertility fight club and helped me to come to terms with my own feelings. It is comforting to know I'm not overreacting or going crazy!

To my friends who have shared my blog posts, put me in touch with people they know, and who have supported this project throughout. They have been there for me throughout my entire infertility process over the last ten years, listening to me whinge and moan and whine. you are the best friends I could ask for and your support means everything to me.

My awesome boyfriend, who has stuck by me for the two years and then some. You supported me throughout this entire writing process, been my proof reader, editor, cover artist and my number one fan. you have been the one helping me to nurture all my rambling typing into something noteworthy. You encouraged me to keep going with it, even when I wasn't sure anyone would notice it. But also for being my partner in all this. There have been a lot of tears and even though I've researched this stuff to the ends of the earth, it's still a daunting. We are still going through this, it is incredibly tough for both of us, but I know with your undivided support we will make it through.

Support and Helpful Links

The Fertility network - The national charity, here for anyone who has ever experienced fertility problems. They have a wealth of information on all aspects of infertility including links to support groups, fertility services, counselling services, and a whole archive of information for couples at all stages in infertility, friends and family, and medical professionals

IVF Babble – The online magazine for all things IVF. Find my column here!

The Miscarriage Association -Miscarriage can be a very unhappy and frightening and lonely experience.
If you have been affected by miscarriage, ectopic pregnancy or molar pregnancy, the miscarriage association is able to help by offering support, impartial information and guidance on all aspects of miscarriage.

HFEA - Human Fertilisation Embryology Association - Basically, if you want reliable facts on the internet about anything to do with fertility treatment, this is the best place to look. The Human Fertilisation and Embryology Authority is the UK's independent regulator, overseeing the use of gametes and embryos in fertility treatment and research.
The HFEA licenses fertility clinics and centres carrying out in vitro fertilisation (IVF), other assisted conception procedures and human embryo research.

BFS - British Fertility Society - Another highly reliable source of information, the BFS has 5 key objectives crucial to infertility provision in the UK:

To promote high quality practice in the provision of fertility treatment.

To provide a common forum for members of various disciplines having an interest in the science and treatment of infertility.

To promote high quality scientific and clinical research in the causes and treatment of infertility.

To provide professional leadership in the provision and regulation of infertility services.

To promote the increase of NHS funding for and equity of access to fertility treatments

Printed in Poland
by Amazon Fulfillment
Poland Sp. z o.o., Wrocław